THE HANDY BOOK OF ARTISTIC PRINTING

10 Cortlandt St., N. Y.

Goodwillie

41 Federal St.,

THE **HANDY BOOK** OF

Artistic Printing

A COLLECTION of LETTERPRESS EXAMPLES

WITH SPECIMENS OF

TYPE, ORNAMENT, CORNER FILLS, BORDERS, TWISTERS, WRINKLERS,

AND OTHER

FREAKS OF FANCY.

BY DOUG CLOUSE AND ANGELA VOULANGAS

PRINCETON ARCHITECTURAL PRESS · NEW YORK

Published by
Princeton Architectural Press
37 East Seventh Street
New York, New York 10003

For a free catalog of books,
call 1.800.722.6657.
Visit our web site at
www.papress.com

Editing: Nancy Eklund Later
Design: Doug Clouse and
Angela Voulangas

Special thanks to: Nettie Aljian, Sara Bader, Nicola Bednarek, Janet Behning,
Becca Casbon, Carina Cha, Penny (Yuen Pik) Chu, Carolyn Deuschle, Russell
Fernandez, Pete Fitzpatrick, Wendy Fuller, Jan Haux, Clare Jacobson, Aileen
Kwun, Linda Lee, Laurie Manfra, John Myers, Katharine Myers, Lauren Nelson
Packard, Dan Simon, Jennifer Thompson, Paul Wagner, Joseph Weston, and Deb
Wood of Princeton Architectural Press   — Kevin C. Lippert, publisher

Library of Congress Cataloging-in-Publication Data

Clouse, Doug.
 The handy book of artistic printing : a collection of letterpress
examples, with specimens of type, ornament, corner fills,
borders, twisters, and other freaks of fancy / by Doug Clouse &
Angela Voulangas.
     p. cm.
 Includes bibliographical references.
 ISBN 978-1-56898-705-7 (alk. paper)
1. Letterpress printing—United States—History—19th century. 2. Graphic
design (Typography)—United States—History—19th century. 3. Type and type
founding—United States—Samples. 4. Printers' ornaments—United
States—Samples. I. Voulangas, Angela. II. Title.
 Z208.C58 2009
 686.2'312—dc22
                              2008039574

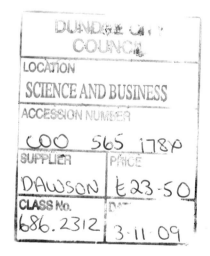

ACKNOWLEDGMENTS

This book could not have come into being without the generosity of the stewards of archives in New York City and New Haven. J. Fernando Peña of The Grolier Club of New York and Jae Jennifer Rossman of the Arts of the Book Collection at Yale University's Sterling Memorial Library helped us to acquire images. Robert Warner of Bowne & Co. Stationers, part of the South Street Seaport Museum, showed us the mechanics, quirks, and possibilities of letterpress printing and made the museum's library available to us. Stephen Saxe was exceptionally generous in opening his home and making his invaluable collection available to curious inquirers. Wayne Furman and David Smith eased research at the New York Public Library.

Friends kindly donated their expertise: Tom McWilliam tutored us in photography; Paul D'Agostino and, especially, Robert Wright, provided photographic ingenuity; Sam Markham led us to image sources; Rita Jules entered text corrections; and Diane DeBlois at the Ephemera Society of America introduced us to helpful collectors of artistic printing. Steven Heller kindly offered advice and inspired us to persevere.

Finally, while we know how fiercely independent nineteenth-century America believed itself to be in matters of artistic printing, these two Americans are greatly indebted to the British Printing Historical Society for having faith in our project and awarding us much needed funds to continue.

This chapter head from *Bright and Happy Homes: A Household Guide and Companion*, by Peter Parley, Jr., (1881), represents artistic printing's predilection for borders, compartmentalized pattern, and in-filled ornament.

The modern, layered arrangement of ornamental borders (overleaf left), culled from the *Printers' International Specimen Exchanges* (1880–98), would likely have been viewed as ill-considered and unfinished to the nineteenth-century eye. Similarly, a page from *Specimens of Printing Types, Borders, Cuts, Rules, &c.*, by the MacKellar, Smiths & Jordan type foundry (1868; overleaf, right) and featuring ornament ganged up and arranged for selling, seems oddly composed by today's standards.

Beautiful

Ornament

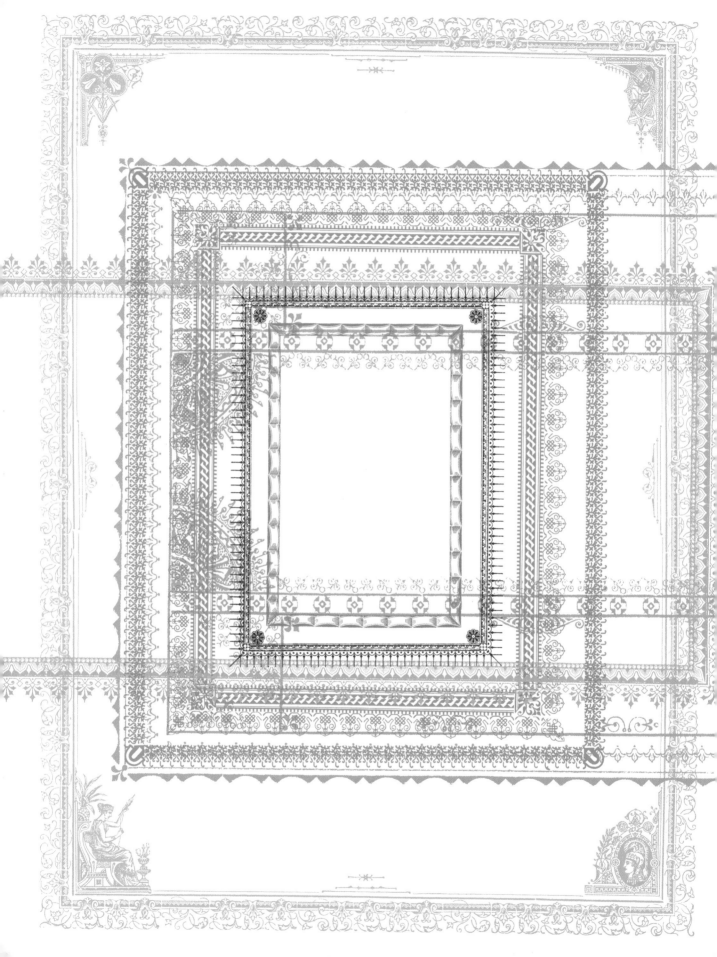

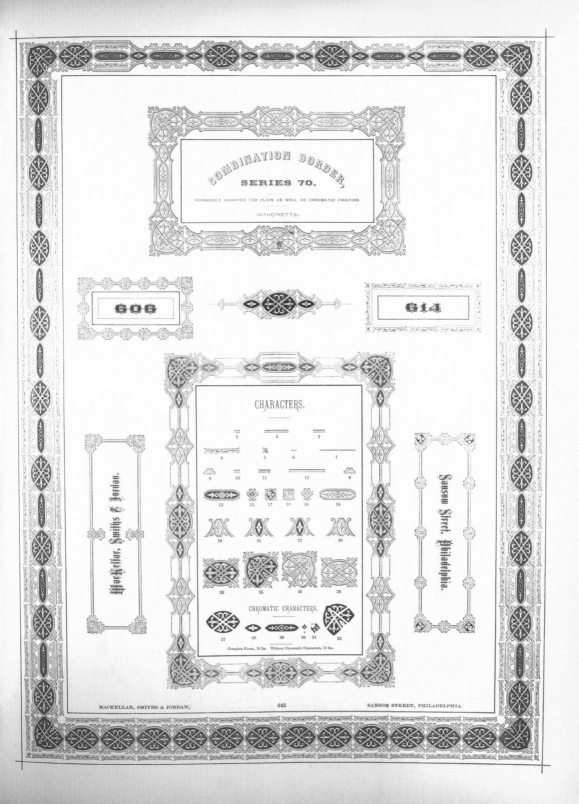

COMBINATION BORDER,

SERIES 70.

ADMIRABLY ADAPTED FOR PLAIN AS WELL AS CHROMATIC PRINTING.

MINIONETTE.

606

614

CHARACTERS.

CHROMATIC CHARACTERS.

Complete Fount, 20 lbs. Without Chromatic Characters, 15 lbs.

Introduction

Artistic printing, a decorative style of letterpress printing dense with ornamental typefaces, unusual compositions, and quirky embellishments, flourished in the late-nineteenth century. It was used primarily to create the ephemera of everyday life—the ubiquitous letterheads, trade cards, advertising circulars, labels, programs, and bills that served an immediate purpose and then just as quickly disappeared into the trash bin or the gutter.

The job printers who created, typeset, and then printed the compositions were in certain respects the predecessors of today's graphic designers. They produced some of the most remarkable graphic work of their century. Stepping away from traditional printed composition, artistic printers of the 1870s and 1880s created with a freedom that would not be matched until the formal and typographic experimentation of the early twentieth-century avant-garde. Prior to the heyday of artistic printing, job printers held fast to the respected methods and conservative values that had been in place since the invention of movable type some four hundred years before. Given this entrenchment, artistic printing's deconstruction of the conventions of the craft is all the more intriguing.

Despite its name, "artistic" printing gained popular success in the commercial arena, rather than within the rarified world of fine art. With the wild growth of manufacturing, new modes of transportation, and rapidly expanding trade, new forms of printed material were required. Laregely, letterpress job printers answered those

The job printing shop of the *Russell Record* newspaper, featured in this 1910 photograph, looks essentially identical to the small job offices of the preceding twenty or thirty years. No presses are actually visible, but type cases are set up in front of the windows, proofing tables are located to the right, and a guillotine paper cutter is placed near the back wall.

11

needs, executing a tremendous portion of the nineteenth century's commercial printing.

Not only did printers have more work than ever before, they had more and better tools with which to produce it. Job printers exploited the technological innovations of the industry, employing them all in an effort to increase the attractiveness of their commercial work by making it more "artistic." Experimentation and novelty reigned, and for a relatively brief moment in the 1880s, artistic printing dominated the printing industry and became, in effect, part of the popular taste.

So how is it that, in the decade that followed, artistic printing fell so precipitously out of fashion? A paradigm of the late-nineteenth-century mania for decoration, artistic printing's ebullience fueled surprisingly volatile controversy. By century's end, it was denounced in outrageously purple prose as "degraded" and "outlandish." Indeed, artistic printing provoked some of the most virulent and extreme judgments of any historical style.

By the early twentieth century, after ornament itself had become morally suspect, artistic printing was laughed into obscurity. Artistic printing has been routinely omitted from historical surveys of graphic design, meriting at most a digressive paragraph.[1] It has been touched upon in studies of printed ephemera, but only one book devoting an entire chapter to the subject is currently in print.[2] Furthermore, most scholars who have considered artistic printing at all have commonly told the story from a British perspective.[3] *The Handy Book of Artistic Printing* corrects this historiographical omission and geographical bias. It concentrates on the style as manifested in the United States in part due to the vitality of the American work, but also because this country generated many of the technological innovations that gave rise to the style and paradoxically hastened its demise. In doing so, this book expands scholarship about an episode in graphic design that has been virtually lost in generalizations about the nineteenth century.

The study of artistic printing provides much needed context for the current interest in ornament. Contemporary graphic design exists in a period of openness not unlike that of the late-nineteenth century. Unremitting technological pace encourages new forms and alternative considerations, tempered with a renewed emphasis on craft and the handmade. In the midst of this is the return to fashion of letterpress printing processes. Ornament abounds. Experimentation is a given. All past styles, from medieval to modernist, and including that of artistic printing, are mined for inspiration in the search for the "new."

Design is cyclical, moving from openness to dogma and back, albeit in pendulum swings that are briefer than ever. Where are we now on that arc, and what lies ahead? This *handy* story of artistic printing's rise and fall from grace provides a context for further investigation.

Compositors are shown choosing type from the cases in this illustration (above) from John Southward's *Modern Printing* (1900). A large composition, such as the cover of the *American Model Printer* (1881; opposite), might involve fitting together hundreds of individual pieces of type and ornament.

12

The American Model Printer.

DEVOTED TO INTERESTS OF THE TYPOGRAPHIC ART AND KINDRED TRADES.

Kelly & Bartholomew,
22 College Place, New York.

CONTENTS OF THIS NUMBER.

"I am soulfully intense

CHAPTER I

Becoming "Artistic"

Artistic printing was only one aspect of a movement in the nineteenth century to make the decorative arts—and life in general—more "artistic." At a time characterized by great uncertainty about style, in which questions of taste were hotly debated, "artistic" telegraphed a heightened sensitivity to beauty and an enlightened or informed engagement with design culture. Taste—what it was, and who had it—was social currency.

Anxieties about the style and quality of manufactured goods plagued designers and manufacturers alike from the 1830s on. Early reformers in Britain attempted to initiate and improve design education, and to strengthen the ties between designers and manufacturers. International exhibitions of manufactured goods highlighted these efforts and placed national accomplishments in the spotlight.

London's Great Exhibition of the Works of Industry of All Nations of 1851 was perhaps the grandest and most provocative event amid the design reforms of the nineteenth century. Under the stewardship of Prince Albert himself, the storied exhibition housed in the Crystal Palace became an enormous financial and popular success. To leading reformers such as Owen Jones, Richard Redgrave, and Matthew Digby Wyatt, however, the Great Exhibition also revealed, very publicly, the short-comings of British manufactured goods. These reformers were dismayed by lack of design principles and the profligacy of mechanically produced ornament on display in the endless glut of gilded mirrors, Persian carpets, Parian statues, rosewood

Created around 1881, this lithographed trade card parodies the aesthetic movement. The swooning figure and saying are based on Gilbert and Sullivan's highly fashionable operetta *Patience*, which opened in New York in 1881.

15

Figure 1
Fourdinois sideboard, featured in the catalog of the Great Exhibition of the Works of Industry of All Nations of 1851
This massive 17-foot-high French sideboard caused a sensation at the Great Exhibition. Its celebrated design and naturalistic decoration carved in deep relief and representing the foods of the world influenced furniture manufacture for decades. It also epitomized what design reformers wanted to change.

furniture sets, fancywork cushions and even a heating apparatus shaped as a suit of armor. What they saw spurred on their efforts to impose some kind of order to the chaos. (*Figure 1*) Reformers maintained that good taste could be acquired through the study of nature, art, and color, and from the considered examination of ornament from sources as diverse as Assyrian architecture and Maori tattoos. (*Figure 3*) In contrast to the taste that characterized many of the objects on view at the Crystal Palace, reform taste would be "artistic."

Beginning in the 1860s, the word "artistic" became associated with the aesthetic movement, an interweaving of art historical theory, scientific study, and commerce that affected all aspects of the decorative arts, architecture, and fine arts. The aesthetic movement was guided by a belief in the power of design and art to express and affect emotional states. It is most closely associated with the work of British designers and writers such as Christopher Dresser, Edward William Godwin, and Charles Eastlake, and the outsized personas of Oscar Wilde and James Abbott McNeill Whistler. Design of the movement was characterized by eclecticism and exoticism, with a special reliance on Japanese, Moorish, Chinese, and Egyptian motifs and an abundance of geometricized natural forms. Art was deemed valuable as an achievement in and of itself, without social or moral justification. "Art for art's sake" was enough.[1]

Because design reformers sought to improve the state of manufactured goods, reform-influenced design was, by definition, concerned with mass production and commerce. "Artistic" became, in turn, a fashionable word that manufacturers—especially makers of domestic decorative goods—readily attached to their products in an attempt to promote sales. (*Figure 2*)

The aesthetic movement and its related ideals of reform spread from Britain to the United States through books such as Charles Eastlake's tremendously successful 1872 American edition of *Hints on Household Taste* (originally published in Britain in 1868), and through events such as the 1876 Philadelphia Centennial Exhibition and the highly publicized lecture tours of Dresser and Wilde. The embrace of aesthetic reform by consumers in the United States emboldened manufacturers and tradesmen to satisfy market demand with a loosely interpreted notion of the "artistic." Despite the commercial opportunism, it appeared that America was at last treating design considerations as a serious matter.

The letterpress-printing industry in particular welcomed both the aesthetic and commercial developments. What became known as "artistic printing" began to develop just as new press innovations, brighter and faster-drying inks, and experimental printing techniques allowed for more flexibility in this particular subset of the printing craft. Neatly adopting the influx of aesthetic and reform styles into the American marketplace, artistic printing joined a loose confederation of new styles with an embrace of new technology, a competitive national spirit, and a reaction against the past.

16

below: **Figure 2**
Furniture advertisement for Jackson & Co., 1880
Design-reform principles blossomed with the aesthetic movement and extended to all household items, furniture, and decoration.

right: **Figure 3**
"Lady's chairs in the Gothic style and early Greek style," from *Principles of Decorative Design*, by Christopher Dresser (before 1873)
Although British reformers such as Dresser stressed function and formal structure, they did not neglect ornament altogether.

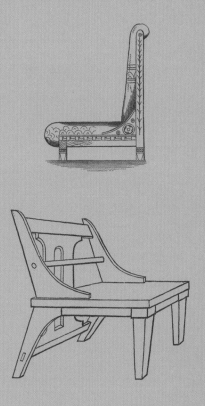

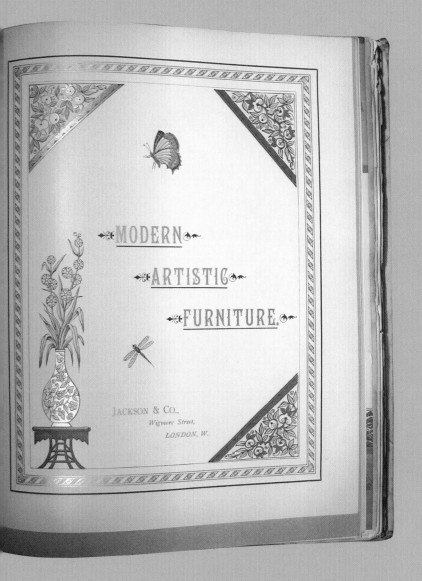

17

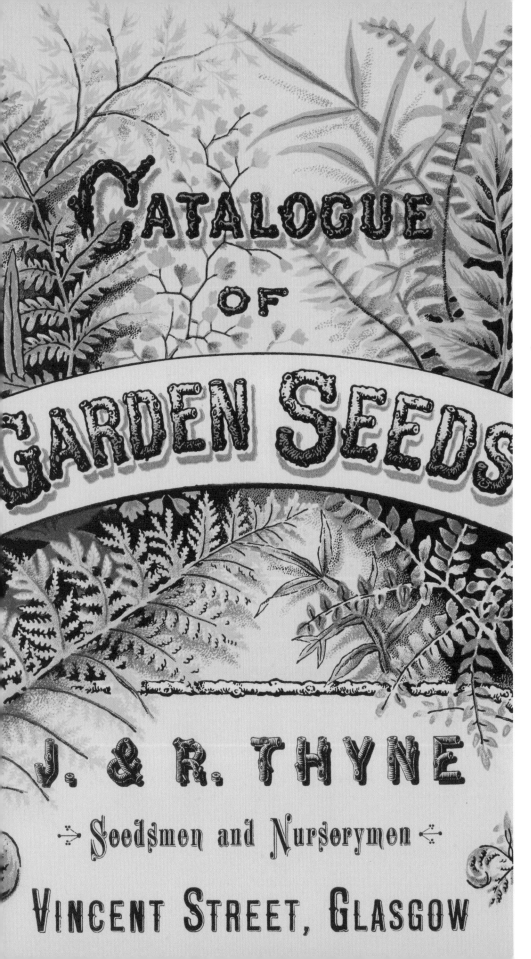

CATALOGUE OF GARDEN SEEDS

J. & R. THYNE

Seedsmen and Nurserymen

VINCENT STREET, GLASGOW

left: **Figure 4**
Catalogue of Garden Seeds, by
J. & R. Thyne, 1886
Hand drawn directly onto stone
blocks (or later, metal plates),
lithographed designs such as this
example freely integrate type and
image. Job printers attempted to
rival lithography's showy effects
in letterpress.

opposite: **Figure 5**
**Advertisement for E. Leipziger's
Temple of Fashion, ca. 1860s**
Characteristic of an earlier style
of letterpress job printing, this
advertisement features stacked,
centered lines of text, set in
several different typefaces and
"filled out" to the width
of the column.

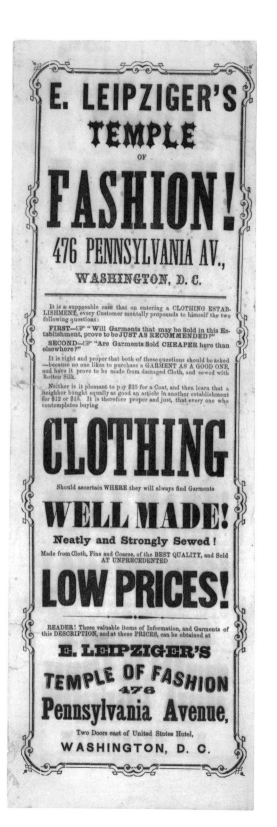

Letterpress printing's primary competitors were lithography and engraving. Invented around 1800, lithography made impressions from designs drawn on stones, or, later, on metal plates. Chromolithography, thought to have been developed in the 1830s although its exact origins are disputed, allowed printing in several colors, using a different stone or plate for each. By midcentury, the latter had become very popular for advertising and packaging.[2] Because lithographers' designs were hand drawn, they could be fluid and extremely decorative, with tightly integrated type and ornament. (*Figure 4*) Similarly, the engraving process employed the use of metal or wood plates that were incised by hand and thus could also reproduce freeform decorative type, ornament, and images.

Letterpress printers felt compelled to compete with the detail, color, and exuberance of these other processes, which were composed freely in two-dimensional space, unrestricted by the fixed axes of their medium. Prior to the mid-nineteenth century, letterpress printing was largely monochromatic—the "everlasting black" of the previous century.[3] Heavy in "fat face" types and closely packed lines, designs mixed several typefaces in single compositions; posters, circulars, and title pages filled space with centered lines that changed size and typeface at each line. (*Figure 5*)

The rivalry that developed between lithographers, engravers, and letterpress job printers is the cause of much of the formal exuberance and experimentation of artistic printing from the late 1860s into the 1890s. Developments in American typefounding techniques gave letterpress printers a decisive boost, and choice in ornamented typefaces exploded. Type foundries had always been integral to the enterprise of letterpress printing and, as sources of typefaces, ornament, and other physical accoutrements of the printing craft, played critical roles in matters of style. Before midcentury, most type was cast by hand in molds, which made it difficult to create letters in thin, delicate strokes. With the invention and refinement of automatic type-casting machines in the 1840s and 1850s, which allowed molten lead alloy to be molded into ever more delicate designs, type became more ornamental.[4] The technology used to create the molds themselves devel-

19

oped so that original designs once necessarily carved by hand in steel could be cut more easily in soft lead alloy. This facilitated the pirating of typefaces from other foundries. Until the late 1860s, American type foundries copied European designs, but they gradually began casting their own original typefaces. Intense competition among American foundries ensued, and each exploited the more sensitive techniques to produce typographic ornament of every form, from decorative corners and flourishes to small landscape scenes. These ornament families, called "combination borders," offered alternatives to the geometric and floral motifs of woodcut and engraved illustrations that had previously constituted printers' stock-in-trade. By the 1870s, combination borders and ornament became distinguishing characteristics of artistic printing.

Letterpress printers readily adopted the seminal motifs and design elements of the aesthetic movement. With the opening of trade with the Far East at midcentury, exotic goods had appeared for the first time in large numbers in the West, where they quickly became the object of much fascination. Japanese and Chinese decorative elements joined Egyptian, Assyrian, and Moorish ones as raw material for inspiration and direct imitation. Compositional strategies such as asymmetry and orientation of elements on the diagonal, were also incorporated, and became strongly associated with the aesthetic movement. And specific motifs such as fans, sunflowers, and peacocks, and even certain shades of color, such as pale green and yellow, were so regularly employed that they became symbols of the aesthetic

sensibility in artistic printing just as they had in interior decoration, fashion design, and painting.

Certain events increased the popularity of British aestheticism generally, and of the Japanese style in particular, in America. In 1876, exhibitors at the Centennial Exposition displayed Japanese wares on U.S. soil for the first time. Two Gilbert and Sullivan comic operas about aestheticism and Japan—*Patience, or Bunthorne's Bride* and *The Mikado*—opened in New York in 1881 and 1885, respectively, and became wildly popular: so popular, in fact, that many businesses appropriated images and phrases directly from the plays. (*Figures 6, 7*)

But until the advent of Japanese combination borders, letterpress printers could not meet the demand for Asian styling as easily as could lithographers, who produced countless trade cards, albums, gift books, and advertisements in a flurry of what was termed the "Japanesque." (*Figure 8*) Because lithographers worked designs freehand, they could recreate the complex, interwoven Japanese motifs quickly, in response to demand. Letterpress printers either had to buy or com-mission engravings, or wait for type foundries to design, cast, and distribute the new Japanese styles. Sometimes letterpress printers would imprint stock Japanese-style trade cards for local businesses, blurring the boundaries between letterpress and lithography (*see Figure 6*). Once type foundries released Asian styles in the late 1870s and 1880s, letterpress printers enthusiastically applied them to much of their work. (*Figures 9, 10*)

Another aesthetic-movement motif that directly influenced artistic printing was the British style of

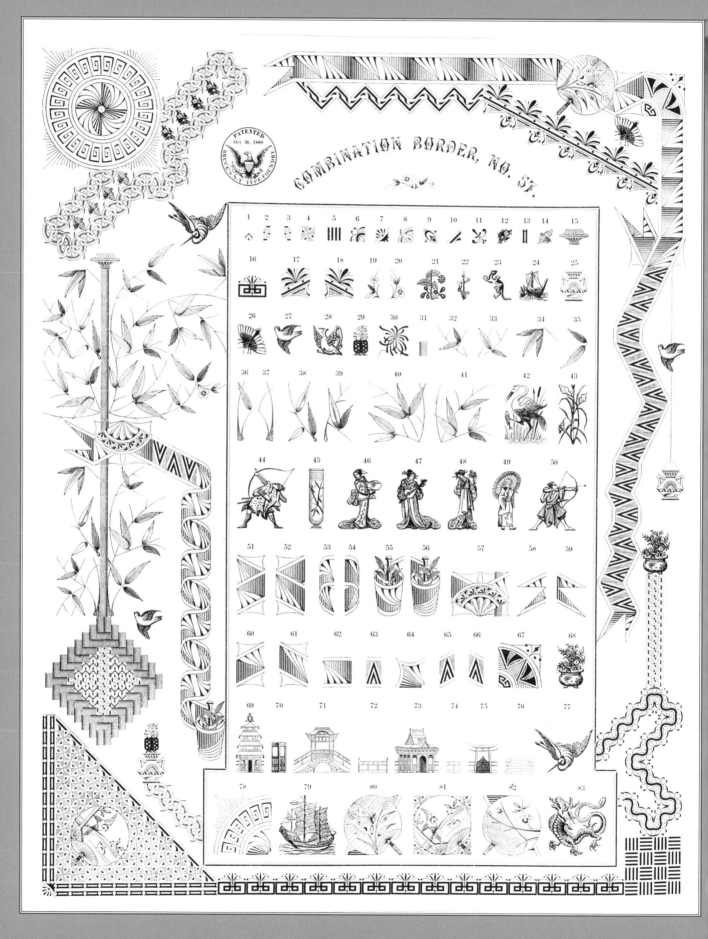

COMBINATION BORDER, NO. 57.

opposite: **Figure 9**
Combination Border No. 57,
by George Bruce's Son & Co.,
1880

right: **Figure 10**
Advertising circular for
Bloomsdale Onions, ca. 1882
This elaborate tableau created out
of scores of individual pieces from
Japanese-, Chinese-, and Egyptian-
style combination border sets
lends an exotic flair to this rather
ordinary item.

top: **Figure 11**
Stylized floral ornament for
stencilling, from Christopher
Dresser's *Studies in Design* (1874)

above: **Figure 12**
Aesthetic-style ornament
on the facade of a Brooklyn
brownstone from ca. 1880

geometricized foliage, called "art botany." Designers of art-botany motifs analyzed plants to discover underlying universal geometric structures and patterns, designs that embodied the unity and variety of natural forms.[5] Developments in theories of evolution and the nineteenth-century compulsion to collect and categorize influenced art botany, which was driven by a search for ideal "types" and systems that unified the bewildering variety found in nature.[6] British design schools used art botany to teach drawing skills and sharpen students' perception of compositional structure.[7] Christopher Dresser, star product of the Government Schools of Design and a respected botanist, became the best-known advocate of art-botanical ornament, which he deftly applied to wallpaper, furniture, and ceramics.[8] (*Figure 11*) Art-botany ornament, and related linear patterning that reworked older, non-figural decoration, surfaced in architecture and design of the 1870s and 1880s. (*Figures 12, 13*) Dresser-like designs in the form of angular, symmetrical branches, stalks of flowers, and sunflowers were easily translated by type foundries into metal typographic ornaments and engravings and then used in artistic printing. (*Figure 14*)

The aesthetic movement, technological innovations, and commercial competition all fostered the beginnings of letterpress experimentation, but it was a printer in Cincinnati, Ohio, who helped distinguish and promote artistic printing. Oscar H. Harpel (b. 1828) published his influential 1870 book *Harpel's Typograph, or Book of Specimens* as a manual for printers. Filled with advice and inspirational samples, an industry critic noted that the *Typograph* had "the effect of starting American printers on the path of progress and emulation that has since borne such magnificent results."[9] Harpel imagined the book might sell well enough outside the printing trades that it could become "an ornament to the centre-table"—the nineteenth-century equivalent of a coffee-table book. He took great care to make it a showpiece, using several colors and a multitude of typefaces and ornaments. (*Figures 15, 16*) In America, the book became a standard addition to printers' libraries, and it was sold by type foundries and offered as a prize at speed-typesetting competitions.[10]

left: **Figure 13**
Table with planter, by Bradley and Hubbard Manufacturing Company, ca. 1880–85
With its tall sunflowerlike spindles, angular "fins," and geometric flora, this art brass planter is the epitome of aesthetic movement styling.

right: **Figure 14**
Advertisement for Geo. Mather's Sons Printing and Lithographing Inks, 1881
Job printers filtered design trends popular in other decorative arts through their own "artistic" sensibility.

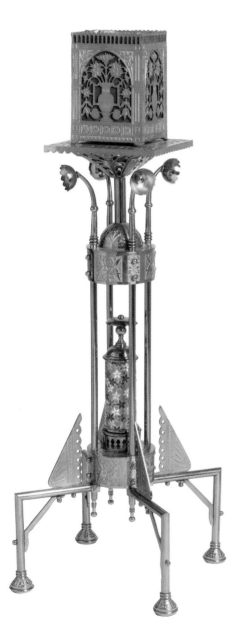

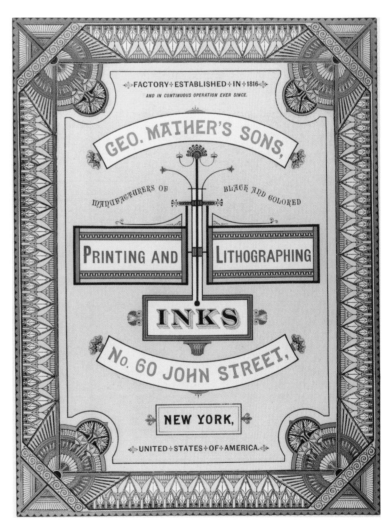

÷FACTORY÷ESTABLISHED÷IN÷1816÷
AND IN CONTINUOUS OPERATION EVER SINCE.

GEO. MATHER'S SONS,
MANUFACTURERS OF   BLACK AND COLORED
PRINTING AND   LITHOGRAPHING
INKS
No. 60 JOHN STREET,
NEW YORK,
÷UNITED÷STATES÷OF÷AMERICA÷

below: **Figure 15**
Harpel's Typograph, or Book of Specimens Containing Useful Information, Suggestions, and a Collection of Examples of Letterpress Job Printing Arranged for the Assistance of Master Printers, Amateurs, Apprentices, and Others (1870), title page

opposite: **Figure 16**
Sample spreads from
Harpel's Typograph

Oscar H. Harpel's meticulously conceived book showcases elaborate letterpress job printing. It served as a style guide for the industry and is credited with spreading the artistic printing movement.

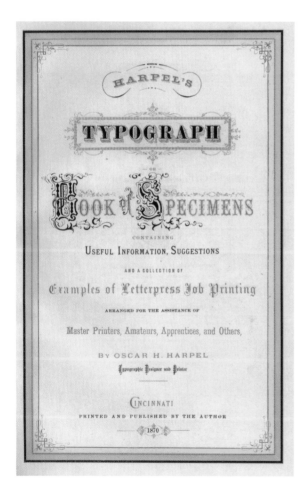

The *Typograph* featured the best American letterpress design of the time, established an industry-wide standard of style, and demonstrated to printers how ambitious they could be.

The craftsmanship of Harpel's specimens is indeed impeccable. Each was characteristically ornamented, many with flourishes inspired by penmanship, and used the typefaces popular at the time—a mix of Gothic, delicate Roman, and early sans serif styles.[11] Fond of borders, Harpel framed every page of text with colored rules and diverse corner embellishments.[12]

His design for the *Typograph* and the specimens he highlights imply a connection between artfulness, quality, and ornamentation, a suggestion that reflects the prevailing assumption among printers that ornament added value to design. Although Harpel believed that ornamented design, which required skillful craftsmanship and took more time to create, signaled artistry and high quality, he had a practical side that shunned ornate work if it was not called for by the job or by the client, or was inartistic or badly crafted. This apparent contradiction between the call for artistry and the precedence of commercial priorities is typical of an age when design was often in the hands of businessmen.[13]

A rival claimant as originator of artistic printing was printer and editor William J. Kelly (b. 1837), who contended that he initiated the style when he began working in New York in the 1860s or 1870s.[14] In one of his own publications, Kelly was described with Barnumesque bombast as "the Homer, the creator, of the poetry of fine printing. . . [a] Phidias in the strength and boldness of his work," and he was lauded as an enthusiastic advocate for artistic printing.[15] A consummate self-promoter, he set up a model American printshop at the sprawling 1878 Exposition Universelle in Paris. Within a year, upon his return to New York, Kelly founded the magazine *American Model Printer* with printer William H. Bartholomew. After closing down this journal in 1887, he began a new one, with C. E. Bartholomew—the *American Art Printer*, which was published until 1893. The indefatigable Kelly later became an editor of the renowned Chicago trade publication the *Inland Printer*.[16]

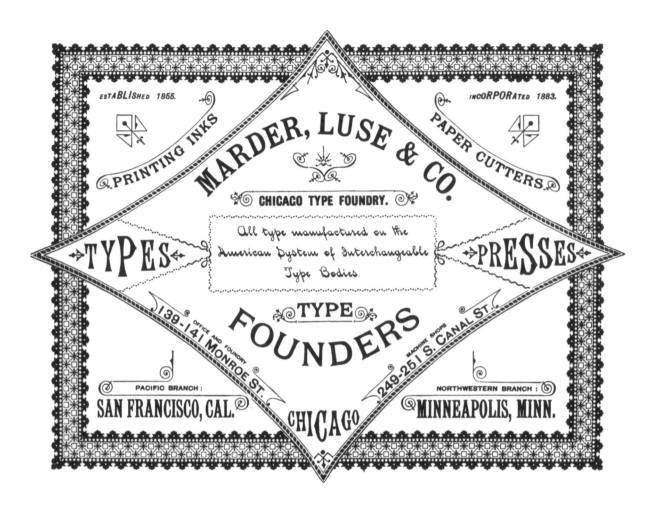

THICK SETTLED HAMLETS CLUSTER ROUND THE SILVERY LAKES AND STREAMS OF LIGHT

WHILE THICKLY STUDDED STARS ABOVE DWELL IN THE AZURE SKIES AT NIGHT

top: **Figure 17**
Advertisement by the Marder, Luse & Co. type foundry, 1884

center: **Figure 18**
Type specimen showing novelty setting

left: **Figure 19**
Trade card of J. F. Earhart, 1883, employing elaborate color effects

opposite: **Figure 20**
Type specimen experimenting with size

Artistic printers regularly pushed the limits imposed by the grid-bound structure of letterpress printing. Executing curves, diagonals, and other typographic gymnastics required dedicated effort and ingenuity, as did employing a multitude of colors.

28

Harmonious TYPOGRAPHY

The *American Model Printer* offered opinions and advice on design, samples of artistic printing accompanied by detailed reviews of the specimens, and analyses of the differences among artistic-printing practices in the United States, Britain, and Europe. This and other American printing-trade journals, such as *Art Age* (1883–89) and *The Superior Printer* (1887–88), encouraged artistic aspirations as a means both to commercial success and to raising the entire trade of printing to an art form. The more printers could appear to defy the limitations of their craft—the small size of their presses, the horizontal and vertical grid imposed by typesetting, the sheer labor involved in typesetting and printing multiple colors—the more closely they would be associated with the highest aspirations of art. (*Figures 17—20*)

Kelly promoted the development of artistic printing by encouraging printers to educate themselves through the study and imitation of the best printing being done. Many printers already collected specimens of admirable work, and trade journals in both America and Europe accepted specimens for review and display on their pages.[17] Printers would also sometimes gather and bind specimens of their best printing and distribute them as business promotions. In late 1879, an Englishman named Thomas Hailing proposed a plan to distribute specimens on a larger scale by establishing an international subscription service that would produce annual volumes of collected printing samples. Hailing hoped that the scheme, called the *International Printers' Specimen Exchange*, would "unite a few of us together in the bonds of fellowship and in the worship of the beautiful."[18] The original proposal asked printers to submit 202 copies of their work to the offices of the English printer Field & Tuer, who would review the submissions, bind them, and deliver the volumes to subscribers. English subscribers were asked to contribute a shilling, Americans, three dollars.

The *International Printers' Specimen Exchange* was a great success. It produced sixteen volumes between 1880 and 1897 and displayed work from Europe, North America, Australia, and Asia. It inspired the formation of other exchanges, in Germany, France, and the United States, among other countries. The *American Printers' Specimen Exchange*, organized by "Ed." McClure in Buffalo, New York, produced four national volumes between 1886 and 1890, and statewide exchanges existed in Ohio and Michigan.

Perusal of the exchanges reveals differences amid the work from contributing countries—differences noted and analyzed by American printing trade journals. Exchange specimens of the 1880s show that American artistic printing was bolder and more structured than much European work, using more and brighter colors and more clearly defined shapes made from well-fitting lines and ornaments. (*Figures 21, 22*) Americans exhibited presses, typefaces, and printed samples in 1877 and 1888 in Britain and in 1878 in Paris, where the consensus—at least according to American journalists—was that American printing was more advanced than British printing. In the 1880s, American typefaces and artistic-printing samples dominated

top: **Figure 21**
Trade card for the Franklin Type Foundry, by J. F. Earhart, reproduced in *The Color Printer* **(1892)**
The international specimen exchanges identified and critiqued characteristic national styles of artistic printing. American printing was known for its vivid use of color, bold design, and twisted and bent rule-work.

above: **Figure 22**
Trade promotion and printing demonstration, by William J. Kelly, 1887

stationers' and printers' exhibitions in London.[19] Because of these successes, Americans claimed, along with the invention of artistic printing, superior craftsmanship and influence over European printing.

Throughout the 1870s and 1880s, Americans criticized British printing, which, they claimed, mixed out-of-date typefaces without regard for composition or emphasis. The *American Model Printer* noted archly that the uniform blandness of British work at least lent it a distinctive character. (*Figures 23, 24*) Americans admired the color and delicacy of German and Austrian artistic printing, though some critics found German work too finicky. Americans found artistic printing from Italy, Spain, and France occasionally promising but lacking in liveliness. (*Figures 25, 26*)

The competitiveness between America and Europe was fueled by the notion that printing styles (like other forms of artistic expression) represented national character. Print design took on a cultural significance that extended beyond the trade. Commentators pitted the Old World against the New, and placed their bets on the latter, which they believed was more likely to advance print design because it had less to lose and was determined to prove its independence from its parent cultures. American work symbolized vigor and freedom from repressive traditions, and the *American Model Printer* suggested that in America even common job printers—or at least those who applied conviction and technology to their personal visions—could create artistic work that was bold, well-crafted, and distinctive, if a little idiosyncratic. Compared to a European tradesman, who was supposedly hampered by the tastes and traditions of older, hierarchical societies, an American printer was characterized as "a thinking man…allowed to exercise this faculty for himself…. [I]n practice he is thorough, methodical and original." American work had supposedly freed itself "from the conventionalities of the grotesque German bordering, and the stiff gawkish taste of England," and the *American Model Printer* claimed that a spirit of

above: **Figure 23**
Advertisement for Morgan & Co.,
photographers and miniature
painters, 1882
Characteristically British is this
example's mix of older faces and
ornament. No single element takes
precedence, giving it a "scattered"
appearance.

right: **Figure 24**
Note head, by Robert Grayson of
the De Montfort Press, reproduced
in John Southward's *Modern*
Printing **(1900)**
The Leicester Free style, or grouped
style, a later incarnation of British
artistic printing, garnered praise
from critics on both sides of the
Atlantic. Its sparer compositions
and artfully staggered lines of text,
set in fewer typefaces, revealed a
greater sensitivity to page layout.

32

independence suffused the work of its citizens, including its printing.[20]

Admittedly, there were faults in America, where "art of all kinds has had to feel the way in almost total darkness and poverty" and where letterpress printers suffered from a lack of design education.[21] Europeans were not all convinced of the quality of American work. One Austrian critic found American artistic printing "distorted in design" and "imbued with American taste-lessness" and claimed to "shudder at the thought" that America might be prescribing a new style.[22]

Criticism that Americans were deviating from good taste was addressed in an 1880 issue of the *American Model Printer*, which eloquently and emphatically stressed that artistic printing did not follow a standard design model and so it was ridiculous to criticize American work for straying from an established style. Beyond submitting to the laws of symmetry, color, light, and shade, printers were completely free to raise their work to art through "individual genial application" and by making the most of their materials and assignments. (*Figure 27*) Printers became artists by being original, and the connection made between artistry and originality was the basis for artistic printing's reputation for novelty.

Some American specimens are naïve and charming, while others, by masters such as A. V. Haight of Poughkeepsie (b. 1842) and J. F. Earhart of Cincinnati (1853–1938), reveal a sophisticated sensibility. Many of the most elaborate specimens were created as promotions for the printing trade, and they demonstrate particular effort on the part of their designers. The development of new press designs, typefaces, inks, and printing techniques had, in effect, handed printers the keys to a cabinet of design curiosities—and possibilities—where artfulness was the only rule.

opposite, top: **Figure 25**
Promotion for the *Cologne Times*, 1886
German printing was recognized as formal, with exquisite coloring and courses of Renaissance- or neoclassical-inspired ornament. It became the most emulated printing mode in continental Europe.

opposite, bottom: **Figure 26**
Bill head for the confectioner Giuseppe Pasqui, ca. 1886
The regal formality of this Italian example owes something to the German style of printing.

below: **Figure 27**
Advertisement for S. B. Hemenway's White Wyandottes, 1887
Even chickens got the "artistic" treatment.

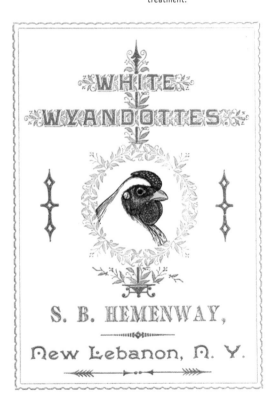

Fig. 86.

CHAPTER 2

Elements of Artistic Printing

To advance out of darkness, heaviness, and crudeness into bright sophistication—that was the intent, at least, as artistic printing came to prominence in the print culture of the 1870s and 1880s. Its decorative eclecticism mirrored its time and was like a graphic distillation of the fashionable quirks apparent in the other decorative arts. Armed with a new, adventurous conception of traditional letterpress printing, artistic printers attempted to balance commercial concerns with creative aspirations, through the use of compositional strategies, typefaces, and ornaments. *(Figures 28–32)*

COMPOSITION

Letterpress printers built up lines of text in hand-held composing sticks (inset) out of individual pieces of metal spacers, leading, and type (such as the display typeface Louis XIV, opposite).

Borders, bands, frames: artistic printing is distinguished by highly idiosyncratic compartmentalized spaces. Moving away from the tradition of centered columns of text surrounded by white space, artistic printing was often built from fields of pattern and color or suggested overlapping geometric shapes. The unexpected and the irregular were favored: extruded diamonds, ovals, lozenges, rectangles with clipped corners, and flared bow ties. Fields required borders, and borders became heavily embellished vehicles for ornament. Artistic printers carved up the architecture of the page with boxes, ribbons, bands, and diagonals, encrusting the framework with

right: **Figure 28**
Settee, advertised on a trade card,
ca. 1880

center left: **Figure 29**
Chair, by George Hunzinger,
ca. 1880

center right: **Figure 30**
Hall stand, by Merklen Brothers,
ca. 1880

bottom: **Figure 31**
"Modern Art" fretwork grille,
by Moses Y. Ransom, from
the Buffalo Grille Co., ca. 1890

opposite: **Figure 32**
Promotion for the Post-Express
Printing Company, 1887

Artistic printing's twisted and crimped rule-work, idiosyncratic shapes, and complexity share a similar sensibility with popular decorative furniture and ornamental woodwork of the time.

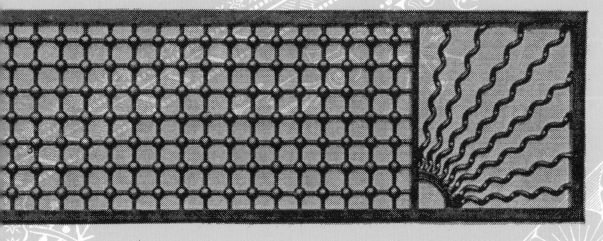

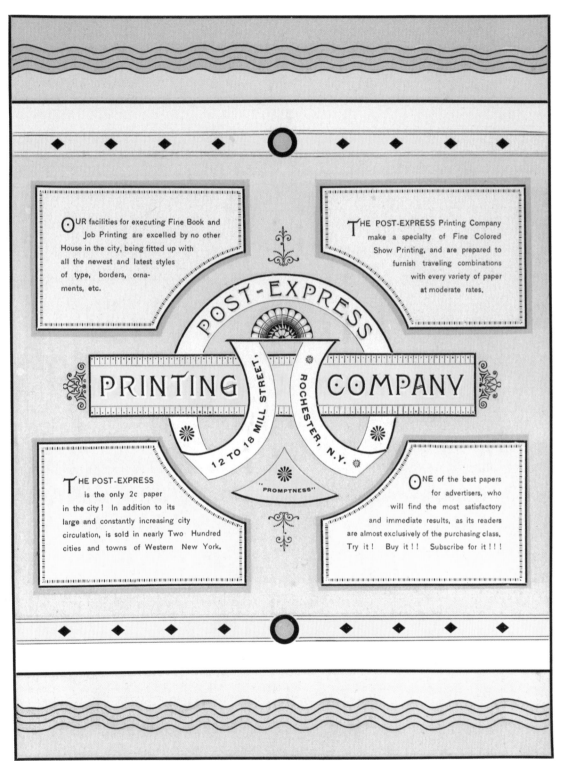

OUR facilities for executing Fine Book and Job Printing are excelled by no other House in the city, being fitted up with all the newest and latest styles of type, borders, ornaments, etc.

THE POST-EXPRESS Printing Company make a specialty of Fine Colored Show Printing, and are prepared to furnish traveling combinations with every variety of paper at moderate rates.

POST-EXPRESS

PRINTING COMPANY

12 TO 18 MILL STREET, ROCHESTER, N.Y.

"PROMPTNESS"

THE POST-EXPRESS is the only 2c paper in the city! In addition to its large and constantly increasing city circulation, is sold in nearly Two Hundred cities and towns of Western New York.

ONE of the best papers for advertisers, who will find the most satisfactory and immediate results, as its readers are almost exclusively of the purchasing class. Try it! Buy it!! Subscribe for it!!!

opposite: **Figure 33**
Assorted corner-fill
ornaments, 1880s
"Corner fills" were typically
nonfigurative and fanlike.
A common conceit of artistic
printing, they also show up
in the architectural carving and
brackets of period woodwork.

left: **Figure 34**
Zig-Zag Combination Border, 1880
The ornament set from which
this detail derives was offered by
the MacKellar, Smiths & Jordan
foundry of Philadelphia. Enormously
popular, it was sold internationally

ornament and filling corner angles with a variety of
fan shapes and spider webs. (*Figure 33*) Diagonal bands
created an impression of asymmetry, though shapes
were often carefully balanced and encased in symmetrical frames. Lines of type were made to curl, arc,
and angle, echoing and filling the odd compositions,
sometimes almost as an afterthought.

The physical requirements of letterpress set it
apart from other printing methods. Engraving and
lithography differed fundamentally from letterpress
in that these processes allowed the drawing of images
and type freehand onto the plates. In letterpress, on the
other hand, elements of metal and wood were built into
an arrangement that had to be "locked up," or secured,
into position. In letterpress printing, even the negative
space on the page required that a physical element be
inserted into the composition. The fact that metal type
was conventionally lined up horizontally and then lines
were stacked vertically imposed a rectilinear discipline.
Diagonal and curved design elements were immediately
more difficult because they had to cross the horizontal
lines of type or spacers. These could not be superim-
posed but rather had to push through each horizontal
line, fitting well enough so that the entire composition could, in order to print, be secured tightly with
space-filling "furniture." (*Figures 34–36*) While type
foundries manufactured specialized tools and spacers
that facilitated the new, ambitious style, some artistic
compositions were so complex or cumbersomely heavy
that they had to be set into plaster, which permanently
locked all the elements into place. Once secured, a particularly successful composition might be electrotyped
(placed in a galvanic solution that created a copper
mold) and duplicated—even changed in size—as a single

top right: **Figure 35**
Diagrams of type set on a
curve from *The American*
***Printer*, by Thomas MacKellar**
(fourth edition, 1868)

Setting type and other elements
on a curve or diagonal within
the axes of letterpress printing
involves a fair bit of ingenuity.

bottom right: **Figure 36**
Metal type and ornament, shown
here in a "lock-up," at Bowne & Co.
Stationers, New York

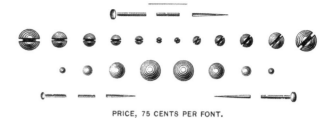

PIN, SCREW AND NAIL HEADS.

PRICE, 75 CENTS PER FONT.

piece of metal, allowing it to be reproduced and disseminated easily. Some trade journals sold electrotyped artistic compositions to augment their income.

As methods of casting improved, type foundries (the suppliers of most printing paraphernalia) were able to offer ornamented type, ornaments, and electrotyped engravings that allowed letterpress printers to design with a delicacy and intricacy approaching that of lithography and engraving, but without having to employ the specialized skills of an engraver or lithographer.

In response to the showy effects produced by lithography and engraving, artistic printing often incorporated the semblance of three-dimensional space even though traditional methods of creating a sense of depth in art—layering and shading—were difficult to execute with letterpress. Artistic printers created the illusion with overlapping shapes and bent corners and used small, sly touches of trompe l'oeil. Ornaments were available that looked like pins that appeared to fasten paper to the background or hold back folded corners. (*Figures 37—39*) Trompe l'oeil painting was extremely popular with the general public in the 1880s and '90s and printers may have picked up on that modish consumer taste as well.

Given this abundance of new materials and the potential newly inherent in letterpress, energized printers paid more attention to design and composition. Early on, *Harpel's Typograph* encouraged its audience to plan the design before setting the type (albeit more as a way to save time than as a strategy for producing the most beautiful design).[1] Trade journals encouraged

sketching before jumping to the composing stick, and displayed how-to guides for the successful composition of elaborately constructed designs. They also endorsed the radical idea of design education for printers—a call answered earlier in Britain than in America.[2]

TYPEFACES

Type foundries had always been integral to the entire enterprise of letterpress printing. In fact, it was the type foundries that held sway in matters of style and taste, because they were the source of typefaces, ornament, and other physical accoutrements of the printing craft. During the second half of the nineteenth century, type foundries became particularly influential by issuing, in increasing volume, typefaces that imitated the extensions and flourishes of penmanship and the eccentricities of engraved type. Once on that path, both type foundries and printers developed a taste for ever more novel and experimental faces. Many foundries produced "fancy" types: designs that became attenuated and grew thin limbs, horns, and "monkey tails," in revolt against the limitations of metal type. (*Figures 40—59*) Some typefaces sprouted whorls, spirals, or delicate pendant curls; others became faceted and geometric. A few combined incongruous characteristics of older designs. These hybrids merged sans serif and serif faces, different kinds of serifs, or highly contrasting thick and thin strokes within one face. Toward the end of the artistic-printing period some typefaces became completely flowing and unstructured, anticipating the art nouveau style.

40

opposite: **Figure 37**
Assorted pin and
nailhead ornaments
Artistic printers frequently
relied on whimsical bits
of visual illusion.

below: **Figure 38**
Pin ornament, in use on
an advertisement for
A. S. Prentiss, Printers

inset: **Figure 39**
Pin ornament, used with
a "torn corner" to create
a trompe l'oeil effect

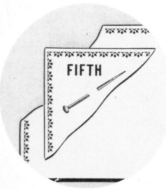

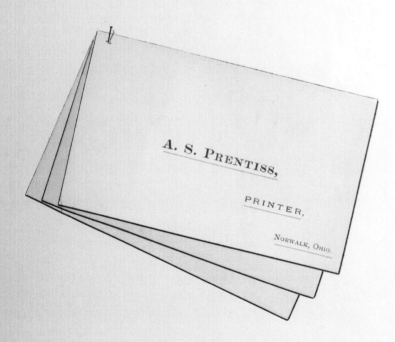

FIGURE 40.
ORNAMENTED NO. 1081, ca. 1885

HOUSE

FIGURE 41. SPIRAL, 1890

PLEASURE

FIGURE 42. UTOPIAN, 1887

FIGURE 43. GLYPTIC NO. 2, 1878

LAND

FIGURE 44. CRITERION, 1884

for

FIGURE 45. CULDEE, 1885

78

FIGURE 46. BARB, ca. 1886

Usefulness.

FIGURE 47. INDESTRUCTIBLE SCRIPT, ca. 1895

FIGURE 48. RELIEVO, 1878

FIGURE 49. RELIEVO NO. 2, 1879

FIGURE 50. FILIGREE, 1878

42

perambulate

FIGURE 51. NOVELTY SCRIPT, ca. 1883

AT

FIGURE 53. MONASTIC, ca. 1879

CROSS ROAD

FIGURE 52. OXFORD, ca. 1887

Customs

FIGURE 54. CRYSTAL, ca. 1890

AM

FIGURE 55. DADO, 1882

CENTRAL

CENTRAL

FIGURE 56. SANTA CLAUS, ca. 1885

GIRLHOOD

FIGURE 57. SCRIBNERS, ca. 1885

Now

FIGURE 58. ZINCO, 1891

is·Hooded·Clouds·like·Friar
their·beads·in·drops·of·Rain
batter·their·doleful·Prayers

FIGURE 59. PENCILINGS, ca. 1885

43

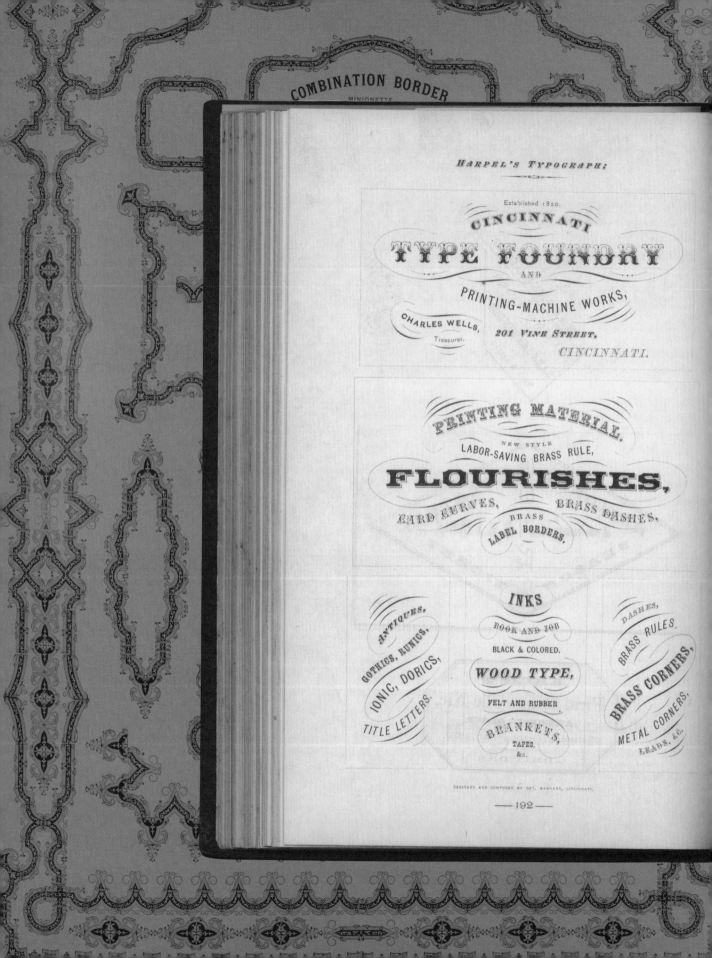

Established 1820.

CINCINNATI

TYPE FOUNDRY

AND

PRINTING-MACHINE WORKS,

CHARLES WELLS,
Treasurer.

201 VINE STREET,

CINCINNATI.

PRINTING MATERIAL,

NEW STYLE

LABOR-SAVING BRASS RULE,

FLOURISHES,

CARD CURVES,   BRASS DASHES,

BRASS
LABEL BORDERS.

ANTIQUES,

GOTHICS, RUNICS,

IONIC, DORICS,

TITLE LETTERS.

INKS

BOOK AND JOB

BLACK & COLORED.

WOOD TYPE,

FELT AND RUBBER

BLANKETS,

TAPES,
&c.

DASHES,

BRASS RULES.

BRASS CORNERS,

METAL CORNERS,

LEADS, &c.

DESIGNED AND COMPOSED BY GEO. BARNARD, CINCINNATI.

—192—

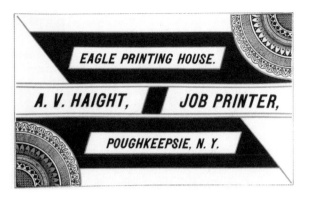

right: **Figure 60**
Trade card for A. V. Haight,
reproduced in the *American*
Model Printer, ca. 1879–82
While artistic printing often
featured several different
typefaces in one composition,
some work was in fact
typographically very spare.

In reaction to the earlier common practice of
"filling out" centered lines of type to a fixed margin
by changing typefaces and type sizes with each line,
artistic printers advocated asymmetric, staggered
layouts. Some artistic printing was, like those earlier
compositions, devoid of restful empty space and packed
with ornament in place of the condensed and Gothic
typefaces of the previous era. Many printers, however,
showed restraint by using only one or two typefaces in a
few sizes. (*Figure 60*)

The most popular artistic typefaces of the time
were made in America. Leading manufacturers
included Marder, Luse & Co., in Chicago; Barnhart
Bros. & Spindler, also in Chicago; MacKellar, Smiths &
Jordan, in Philadelphia; and the Boston Type Foundry.
Certain faces appear repeatedly in artistic work, especially the medievalist Glyptic (1878); the bold, carved
effect of Relievo and Relievo No. 2 (1878–79); Monastic
(1860s); Filigree (1878); and Mural (before 1883). At

least one foundry—MacKellar, Smiths & Jordan—had
agents in England, Australia, and South America, while
other American types (or very similar designs) were
resold by overseas foundries.[3]

ORNAMENT

Artistic printers used two primary kinds of ornament:
metal typographic ornament produced by type foundries, and "homemade" rules and borders they created
themselves by bending and manipulating thin lengths of
brass. Typographic ornaments were immensely popular
in the late 1870s and early 1880s and filled artistic
printing. These sets of tiny metal shapes and images,
called "combination borders," were ingeniously designed
to fit together, puzzle-like, to create frames, dividers,
and containers for type, or as tableaux of exotic scenes
meant to rival custom engravings. Typographic ornament
was plentiful and well developed as early as 1860. One
American type founder's catalog from 1868 shows page
after page of delicate, elaborate borders—neoclassical
patterns, calligraphic florals, rustic latticework—most
of which may in fact have come from Great Britain and
Europe. (*Figures 61, 62*) It was this style of ornament, used
primarily for framing type in dense, intricate thickets,
that was favored by Continental printers and that was
used in early artistic printing in this country. American
ornament took on a completely different, often pictorial, cast; and by the late 1870s, the call for fashionable

opposite: **Figure 61**
Flourishes, from *Harpel's*
Typograph (1870)
Decades older than the *Typograph,*
these midcentury flourishes
replicated the showiness of
penmanship.

opposite, background:
Figure 62
Minionette Combination Border,
ca. 1860s
By the 1870s, Gothic-Revival-style
borders such as these had been
replaced by new releases from
American foundries.

45

Figure 63
Combination Border No. 60, in the Assyrian style, by George Bruce's Son & Co., New York

Neither the Assyrian nor the Egyptian style achieved the popularity of the Asian-inspired borders, which became ubiquitous in the 1880s.

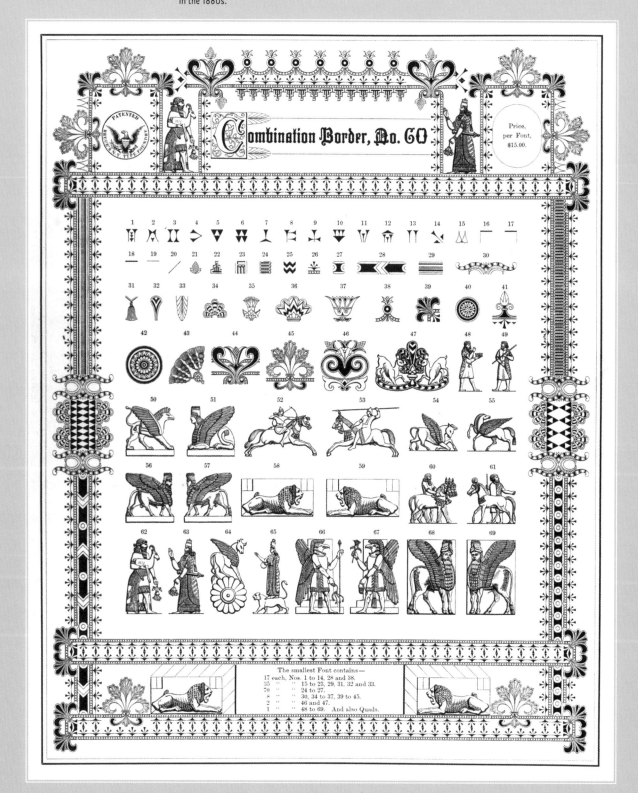

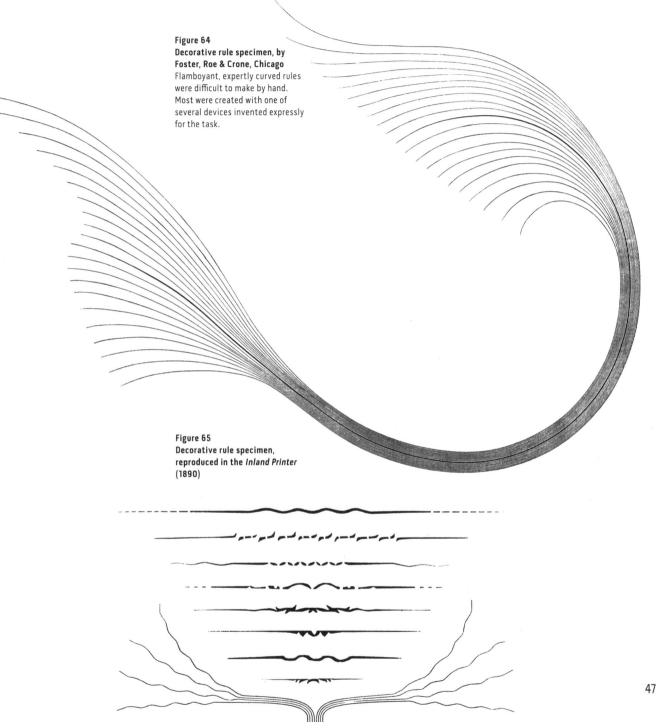

Figure 64
Decorative rule specimen, by
Foster, Roe & Crone, Chicago
Flamboyant, expertly curved rules
were difficult to make by hand.
Most were created with one of
several devices invented expressly
for the task.

Figure 65
Decorative rule specimen,
reproduced in the *Inland Printer*
(1890)

top: **Figure 66**
**Design for an envelope corner,
overlaid with samples of
manipulated rules**
Printers who were industrious, or
who simply did not have the funds
to purchase ready-made ornament,
crafted details like these with a
pair of pliers, or "twisters."

bottom: **Figure 67**
**A rule portrait of George W. Childs,
a printing industry benefactor**
Compositors attempted to show
off their rule-bending skills by
creating portraits and other simple
illustrations.

48

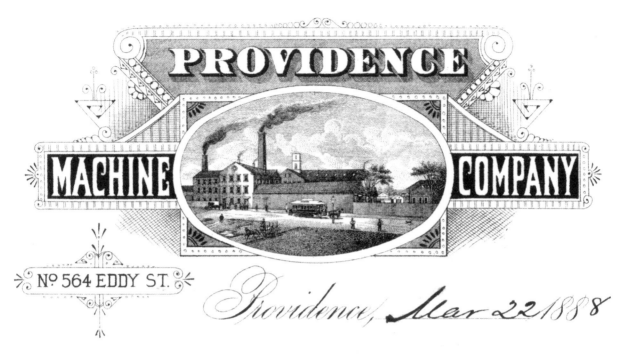

Figure 68
Engraved bill head, 1880s.
Artistic printing's rule-work
was inpired by the fine lines of
engraving.

exotica was answered with sets designed in Japanese, Chinese, Assyrian, and Egyptian styles. (*Figure 63*) The Philadelphia foundry MacKellar, Smiths & Jordan and George Bruce's Son & Co., in New York City, dominated the market.

For about $4 in 1890 (or roughly $91 in 2007), a printer could buy a set of about twenty pieces of Japanese-style ornament.[4] Some fit together to make Asian-inspired patterns; others were discrete illustrations—fans, vases, bamboo, dragonflies, cranes, and frogs. Elements of the Chinese sets could be used Lego-like to build simulations of Chinese bridges and temples. Dragons, pugs, and "Chinamen" on stilts filled these scenes. Egyptian and even Assyrian sets with sphinxes, palms, obelisks, pyramids, and winged bulls could also be purchased.

One of the most controversial (and later ridiculed) practices of artistic printing was its use of brass rules, which were cut and bent into ornaments, diagonals, curves, and even images. (*Figures 64—67*) The inspiration for much rule-work may have come from engraving, which produced very fine lines. (*Figure 68*) Printers could imitate engraving by bending the brass rules—which they had once used to print straight lines—into frames, curves, curls, and ornamented borders. Printers who decorated with bent rules were known as "twisters." Their crimping and bending efforts were supported by specialized mechanisms with names such as the Earhart Wrinkler and the Bartholomew Twister, and by ongoing advice in trade journals.[5] (*Figures 69, 70*) Whereas printers had once depended solely upon type foundries to supply ornaments, they could now create their own with only a pair of tweezers and a length of brass rule. (Some talent for patternmaking and illustration was helpful as well.) The more enthusiastic twisters even went so far

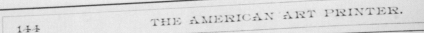

THE BARTHOLOMEW "TWISTER."

Price, $4.00

Price, $4.00

THE COUNTRY PRINTER'S
DELIGHT.

HANDY, POR...
CHE...

NO WAITING IN LINE AT
THE CURVING MACHINE.

CURVING AND TWISTING
A PLEASURE.

*All the Curves and Twists shown
on this page were made with the
Bartholomew "Twister."*

C. E. BARTHOLOMEW,

SOLE MANUFACTURER,

22 COLLEGE PLACE,

NEW YORK, N. Y.

opposite: **Figure 69**
The Bartholomew Twister,
created by Charles E.
Bartholomew, publisher of the
American Art Printer

below: **Figure 70**
The Earhart Wrinkler, patented
invention of well-known printer
J. F. Earhart

Compositors who were particularly
adept at fashioning decorative
rule-work, whether by hand or
with machines such as these,
were called "twisters." Twentieth-
century critics of artistic printing
often saved special ridicule for
the twisters.

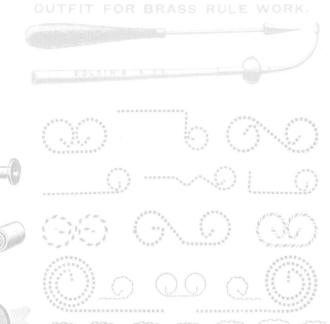

OUTFIT FOR BRASS RULE WORK.

EARHART & RICHARDSON

J. F. EARHART
J. E. RICHARDSON

60 JOHN STREET, NEW YORK, U.S.A.

Factory established and in continuous operation since 1816.

MAKES OVALS, CIRCLES, ETC.

NO TEMPERING OF BRASS.

THE "PRINTER'S" CURVING MACHINE,

KELLY & BARTHOLOMEW,
NEW YORK.
22 COLLEGE PLACE.

FOR SALE BY TYPE-FOUNDERS
EVERYWHERE.
AND GENERAL DEALERS

PATENTED, MAY 19, 1881.

Price,
$15.00.

Compact
and Neat.

MAKES ANY CURVE

RAPIDLY AND TRUE.

FOR BENDING BRASS RULES, LEADS, ETC.

ANY PERSON CAN USE THIS MACHINE.

51

as to create portraits from bent rules. Often clumsy and stiff, shapes made from rules almost always belied their origin in bent metal and rarely matched the flowing freedom of the engraver's art. It is this rule-work that sometimes gives artistic printing the flavor of folk art.

COLOR

Just as printers moved from relative poverty of type and ornament choice to abundance, so they moved from a pallid world of limited color—mostly black, perhaps punctuated with a single primary color—to one of numerous and varied "artistic" colors. Industrial experimentation with coal tar and petroleum additives had radically expanded the range of available pigments, improved color saturation, and shortened drying time. While the selection of inks might prove exciting, even inspirational, the actual printing of colors in letterpress remained laborious.

Artistic-printing specimens regularly used four, five, or sometimes many more colors, and each color required that the paper make a separate pass through the press. Alignment and registration of several colors during separate printing was a sign of excellent craftsmanship, so ambitious printers displayed their skill by printing numerous colors within a single composition. The choice of colors became important and controversial in printers' trade journals—the de facto salons of the industry. Lively, often very technical debates took place about the categorization and description of colors, harmonious combinations, and how to mix them. Journals provided color formulas for popular tints and dissected examples of jobs to discuss the order in which colors were printed and how the combinations were achieved. (*Figures 72–74*)

Color choices sometimes reflected aesthetic taste: the subtle celadons or blues of Japanese prints or sophisticated, nearly murky browns and golds reminiscent of Whistler's tenebrous canvases. Jewel-like carmine red was popular, as were greens, pale blues, and yellows. The most ambitious colorists sometimes

below: **Figure 71**
Specimen of Chaostype, a process patented by J. F. Earhart, 1883

opposite: **Figure 72**
Color wheel, from J. F. Earhart's definitive treatise, *The Color Printer* (1892)

printed in several bright colors that, when combined with Japanese-style ornament, suggested Japanese woodblock prints. Printers experimented with metallic inks and colored or translucent papers, and many appeared to enjoy tinkering with materials and processes. They sought to add texture with novel methods of applying ink to paper and tried printing from cloth, leather, even hair—with varying success. Some of them patented their more successful experiments. Noted printer and colorist John Franklin Earhart (see pages 82, 100, and 130) patented a procedure that he called Chaostype, the printed result of which resembled a cross between marbled paper and luncheon meat. The texture was achieved by printing layers of colored and metallic ink from plates made out of random drips of molten metal. It proved so popular that others experimented with similar processes or mimicked the look outright, and soon artistic printing was rife with Hazotype, Owltype, Cloudtype, and Metamorphic borders. (*Figure 71*)

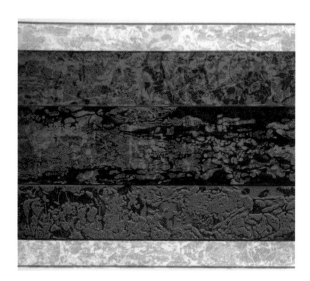

PLATE 32

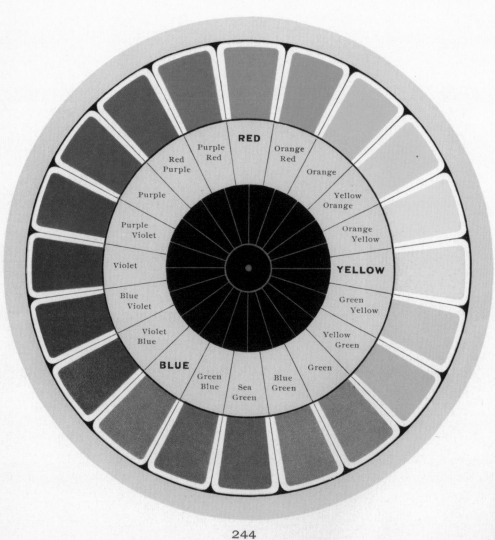

244

Scale of Complementary Colors.

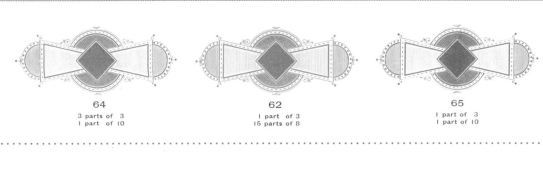

64
3 parts of 3
1 part of 10

62
1 part of 3
15 parts of 8

65
1 part of 3
1 part of 10

BISMARK BROWN

BRONZE BLUE

BUFF

CHERRY LAKE

DRAGON GREEN

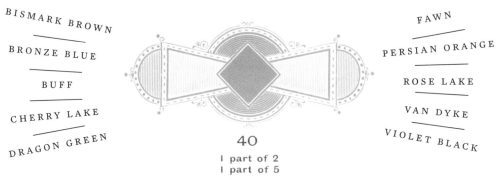

FAWN

PERSIAN ORANGE

ROSE LAKE

VAN DYKE

VIOLET BLACK

40
1 part of 2
1 part of 5

390
Violet-Blue and Green-Yellow

The black was printed first, and then the blue, pink, and yellow tints, in the order named.

Yellow.   Yellow on Blue.   Blue.   Pink on Blue.   Pink.   Yellow on Pink.   Yellow.

FIGURE 73. COLOR SAMPLES FROM J. F. EARHART'S *THE COLOR PRINTER* (1892)

PERSIAN ORANGE, $6.00 (15-442)

SPECIAL FINE BLUE, $4.00 1/2-723

No colour harmony is of high order unless it involves indescribable tints. It is the best possible sign of a colour when nobody who sees it knows what to call it, or how to give an idea of it to anyone else. Even among simple hues the most valuable are those which cannot be defined.... The finer the eye for colour, the less it will require to gratify it intensely. —JOHN RUSKIN, *THE TWO PATHS* (1859)

FIGURE 74. ADVERTISEMENT, AULT & WIBORG INK COMPANY (detail)

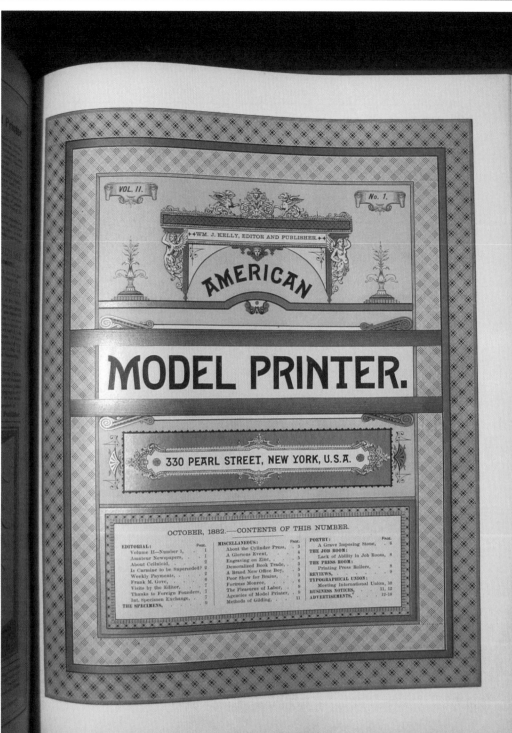

VOL. II.

No. 1.

+ WM. J. KELLY, EDITOR AND PUBLISHER. +

AMERICAN

MODEL PRINTER.

⊛ 330 PEARL STREET, NEW YORK, U.S.A. ⊛

Specimens
of **ARTISTIC PRINTING**

Collected as showpieces, numerous examples of the best artistic printing avoided the fate of most printed ephemera, the trash can, until tastes changed in the twentieth century. A good deal of nineteenth-century paper ephemera made it to the 1940s only to be carted off in the raw-material salvage drives instituted during World War II. Luckily, not all the specimens of artistic printing were hauled away. The specimens reproduced on the following pages range from the stunningly ambitious to the intriguingly flawed. Many are printers' self-promotional pieces, but all represent a stylistic approach that was pervasive in common commercial letterpress printing in the 1880s. Whether parading inspired idiosyncrasy or simple naïveté, each radiates charm, earnest effort, and an air of experimentation.

Some of these pieces do not conform to today's accepted principles of good design; in fact, this portfolio includes a fair bit of "bad" design. Any given work's "badness," however, reveals a spirit of investigation and presents novelties of form once a part of common visual culture but rarely—if ever—reproduced or displayed since their first appearance.

1

Greeting!

Alex J. Robertson, New York

Although it appeared in the *American Printers'
Specimen Exchange* without explanation, this piece
may have been part of a carrier's address—one of
the decorative broadsides or pamphlets put out by
newspapers at holiday time. The addresses were
distributed to subscribers by the carriers in hopes of
receiving a gift in recognition of the year's dependable
delivery. A carrier, it should be noted, was frequently
an apprentice, or "printer's devil."

Striking in its straightforwardness, the shape
creates the illusion of four delicate, origami-like folded
corners. Its very sophisticated color palette features
iridescent, metallic green ink with gold highlights, and
it is printed on a pale lavender paper. The *American Art
Printer* rhapsodized, "It is perfection, and gives a
restful sense of completeness the moment it is seen.
There is not a flaw."

58

MERRY CHRISTMAS!

+1887+

Greeting!

+1888+

HAPPY NEW YEAR!

Alex. J. Robertson, New York.

2

**Advertising blotter
1887**

The Press

The Press Printing and Publishing Company,
Paterson, New Jersey

Job-printing offices of newspapers like *The Press* often took on other commercial assignments in addition to putting out the daily paper. This advertisement reels off typical services offered: circulars, handbills, programs, and letterheads among them.

This handsome advertisement, constructed in a banded style, consists of parallel compartments of color-blocking and ornamental fill. Though the composition is compact and dense and has none of the angled or curved type artistic printers were so fond of, it remains lively for the variety of patterns and red highlights it features. Highly detailed border elements and an engraved medallion give it a European, neoclassical flavor.

Parallel rules and borders set flush up against one another, as they are here, call for rigorous registration at each pass through the press. In this particular example, the red color pass is not quite aligning, resulting in bouncing ornaments and white "cracks."

60

Billheads.
Circulars.
Handbills.

JOB PRINTING

Ball Cards.
Programmes.
Invitations.

The DAILY Press

The Weekly Press

THE ✳ PRESS
Printing & Publishing
Company,
269 MAIN STREET, PATERSON, N. J.

Lithographing
Blank Books.
Envelopes.
Letter Heads.
Note Heads.
POSTERS.
Silk Labels,

3

Charles F. Libbie, Fine Printing

George G. Thayer with Charles F. Libbie, Jr.,
Boston, Massachusetts

An exercise in banner making, this ad has an antic, Rube Goldbergian air about it. It is largely built by hand from brass rules, rather than being composed of manufactured ornaments—which allowed the compositor free rein at "original designing." The resulting flagpole is painstakingly bedecked with fluttering streamers and incongruous sprigs, planted on ground that is virtually curling away. Note the company motto at the lower left: "Not how cheap, but how good." The pennant at the top reads (in translation), "Criticism is easy, and art is difficult."

62

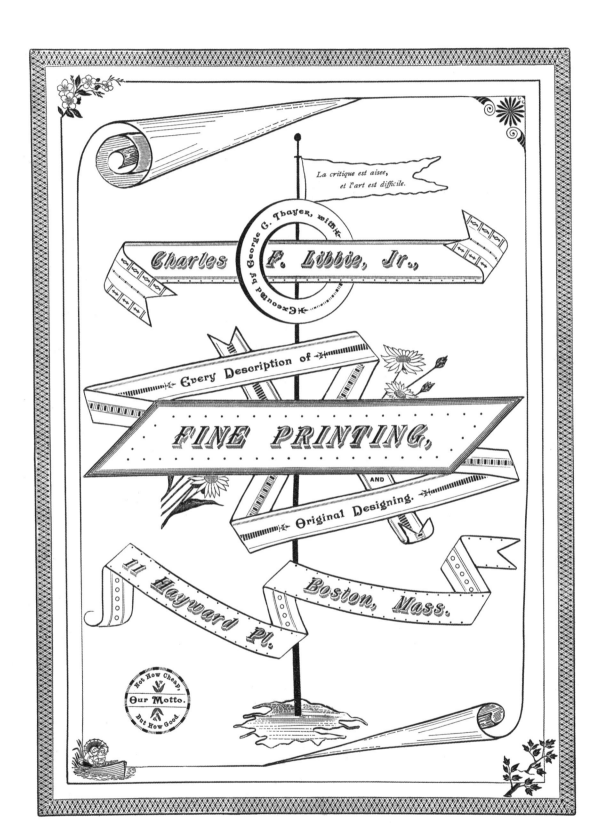

La critique est aisee,
et l'art est difficile.

Charles F. Libbie, Jr.,

George C. Thayer, with

Executed by

Every Description of

FINE PRINTING,

AND

Original Designing.

11 Hayward Pl.

Boston, Mass.

Not How Cheap,
Our Motto.
But How Good

4

Foster, Roe & Crone

Foster, Roe & Crone, Chicago, Illinois

Foster, Roe & Crone, a high-profile printing firm of the late 1880s and early '90s, had a lot of what would today be called "marketing buzz." This advertisement for their "art fake" booklet, an annual self-promotional publication, was extremely well known and circulated widely at the time. The meaning of "art fake" is not completely clear, but the term seems to wink at the issues of authenticity and artistry that were preoccupying the printing world.

The pairing of a bizarre, free-form, textured shape and the very staid business-card composition is pure audacity—and vintage Foster, Roe & Crone. The firm was known for its extravagant curved and "wrinkled" rules, which were widely copied.

The *American Art Printer* frequently discussed Foster, Roe & Crone and once summarized its work as "a rare conglomeration of flashes that nearly amount to genius and aberrations that almost border on madness."

64

Foster Roe & Crone

140-142 MONROE STREET
CHICAGO

SEND FIFTY CENTS IN STAMPS
FOR OUR
ANNUAL ART FAKE BOOK
ONE HUNDRED PAGES THREE TO TEN
COLORS ON EACH PAGE

5

....

Trade promotion
1882

Kelly & Bartholomew,
Fine Art Printers

Kelly & Bartholomew, New York

This trade advertisement is inventive, confident, and skillfully produced despite its odd divisions of space. It was printed by William H. Bartholomew, likely the brother of Charles E. Bartholomew, publisher of the *American Art Printer*. Both Bartholomews were in business with William J. Kelly, the outspoken showman and early promoter of artistic printing.

The advertisement's vivid, saturated colors are reminiscent of the design plates in Owen Jones's extremely influential *Grammar of Ornament* (1856).

WILLIAM J. KELLY

66

KELLY & BARTHOLOMEW,

FINE ART PRINTERS,

22 COLLEGE PLACE, N. Y.

6

West's Improved Memoranda Calendar

George West, Easton, Pennsylvania

George West, who worked out of Easton, Pennsylvania, styled himself "West, the Printer" and contributed several flamboyant pieces to the specimen exchanges. Despite his flare for self-promotion, not much is known about West aside from his impressive samples, which were widely praised and remain fascinating studies in idiosyncrasy today.

One look at this "Improved Memoranda Calendar" immediately makes one wish there was more information to be had about Mr. West. The calendar's slightly disturbing design concept showcases West's own disembodied head with what can only be termed "ear horns," which trumpet self-promotional boilerplate. Deceptively simple-looking, this specimen is somewhat technically advanced in that it features a divided black-and-white halftone of West's printing shop on the main thoroughfare of Easton. The halftone was patented around 1881 but was not commercially viable until the early 1890s, when refinements in the procedure made it an increasingly common illustration method.

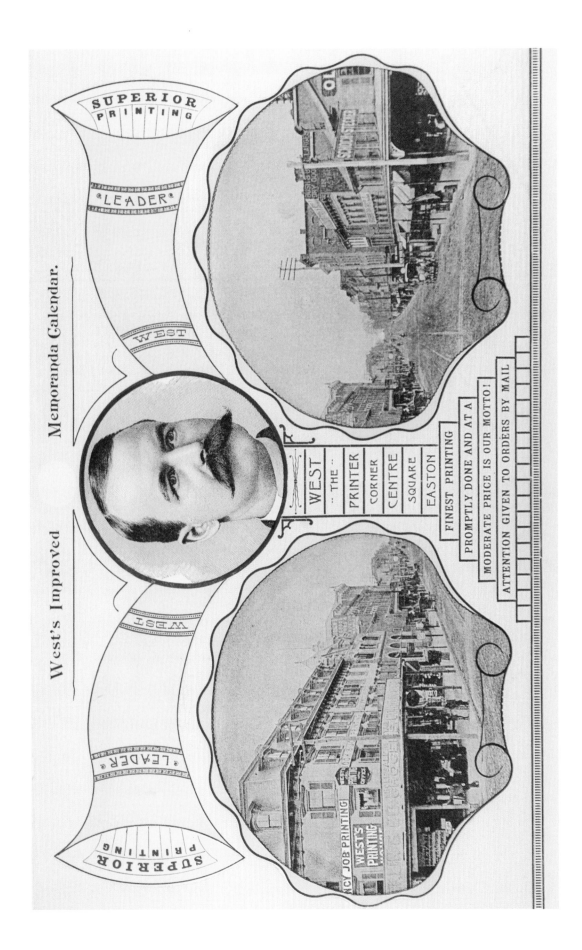

West's Improved   Memoranda Calendar.

SUPERIOR
PRINTING

◦LEADER◦

WEST

WEST
·· THE ··
PRINTER
CORNER
CENTRE
SQUARE
EASTON

FINEST PRINTING
PROMPTLY DONE AND AT A
MODERATE PRICE IS OUR MOTTO!
ATTENTION GIVEN TO ORDERS BY MAIL

7

Advertisement
1885

Brooklyn Eagle

Brooklyn Eagle job shop, Brooklyn, New York

At the time of this advertisement, Brooklyn still had thirteen more years of independence before it made the "Great Mistake" and allowed itself to be incorporated into New York City.

At various points in its colorful 114-year run, the *Brooklyn Eagle* newspaper, founded in 1841, was the nation's most widely read afternoon paper, maintained international offices and had Walt Whitman as its editor. The newspaper got its first steam-powered printing press, or "engine," in 1851, and the job-printing shop was obviously extensive and well established by the time of this ad. It handled a full spectrum of offerings, including book and poster printing, as well as lithography and engraving.

The complicated division of space within this design, where no single element quite takes precedence, is typically "artistic."

8

Trade card
date unknown

Goodwillie, Wyman & Co.

That this is probably an early specimen is evidenced by the lingering presence of Gothic Revival typefaces and the heavy "French Clarendon" numeral—all popular in the 1860s. These elements are nevertheless combined with typical artistic conceits, such as the folded ribbon and the illusion of overlap, even though there is not much in the way of specifically Asian or aesthetic ornament, which were all the rage by 1880 or so. The single corner-fill ornament, a hallmark of the "artistic," appears rather rudimentary. While it is possible that this designer may not have had access to an up-to-date selection of typefaces and ornaments, it is unlikely, considering the business—printers' supplies.

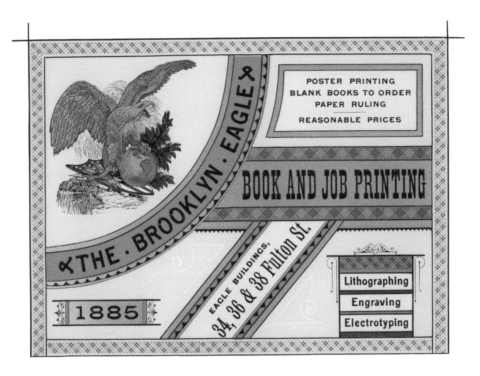

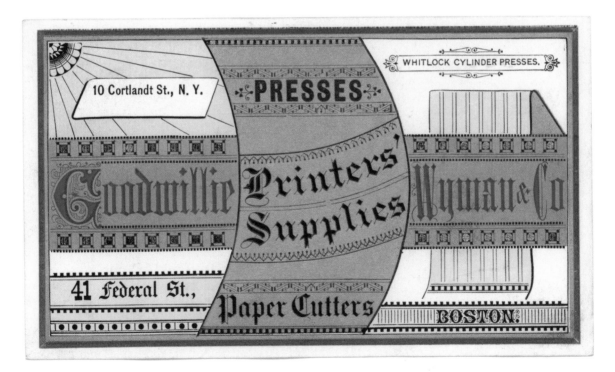

9

Menamin's Printers'
Furnishing Warehouse

Rowley & Chew, Philadelphia, Pennsylvania

Advertisement
1870

As one of the supplements to Oscar Harpel's
celebrated *Typograph*, this advertisement needed to
be especially impressive given the book's goal of
improving print design. Almost ethereally light and
serene, the composition uses relatively unadorned type
in an extremely decorative and labor-intensive way.
The elegant and deftly handled curved text, from the
central dial of concentric rings to the penmanship-
inspired corner flourishes, energizes the symmetrical
composition. The ornament and type do not yet evince
any aesthetic movement or "Oriental" influence but
are artistic in their delicacy, careful craftsmanship,
and geometry.

Of particular note is that Rowley & Chew list
themselves as "Artistic Printers," one of the earliest
instances of that term.

72

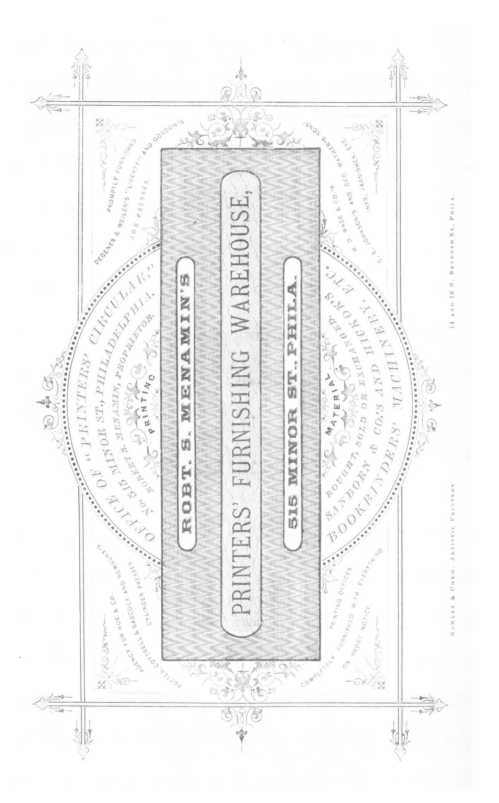

ROBT. S. MENAMIN'S

PRINTERS' FURNISHING WAREHOUSE,

515 MINOR ST., PHILA.

OFFICE OF "PRINTERS' CIRCULAR,"
No. 515 MINOR ST., PHILADELPHIA.
ROBERT S. MENAMIN, PROPRIETOR.

PRINTING

DEGENER & WEILER'S "LIBERTY" AND GORDON'S
JOB PRESSES,
PROMPTLY FURNISHED

AGENCY FOR HOE & CO.'S
POTTER COTTRELL & BABCOCK AND NEWBURY'S
CYLINDER PRESSES

C. E. JOHNSON'S INKS, VARNISHES, ETC.
H. D. WADE & CO.'S AND GEO. MATHER'S SONS.

MATERIAL
BOUGHT, SOLD OR EXCHANGED
SANBORN & CO.'S AND HICKOK'S
BOOKBINDERS' MACHINERY

OLD TYPE, ETC.

PRINTING OFFICES
COMPLETELY FURNISHED WITH EVERYTHING
ON SHORT NOTICE.

14 AND 16 S. SEVENTH ST., PHILA.

ROWLEY & CHEW, ARTISTIC PRINTERS

73

10

....

**Fragrance label
1888**

Florida Water

C. C. Bartgis & Bro., Baltimore, Maryland

The ornament and decorative choices in this fragrance label are completely appropriate to the subject matter and combine to enhance a particular message—a fairly rare instance in artistic printing. The exotic touches create an effective sense of tropical romanticism: ferns and other flora drape languidly from a delicate tracery border above frolicking butterflies and a palm tree. The unusual choice of red as the primary ink color, paired with a neutral pale green and yellow, adds to the implied hothouse air. Less successful is the type encased within confused banding, and the flock of comically undersized birds that resemble gnats.

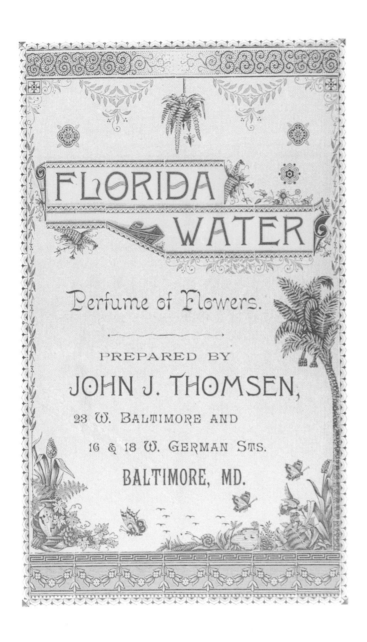

FLORIDA WATER

Perfume of Flowers.

PREPARED BY

JOHN J. THOMSEN,

23 W. BALTIMORE AND

16 & 18 W. GERMAN STS.

BALTIMORE, MD.

11

·····································

**Memorial souvenir
for John and
George Grady
1886**

In Memoriam

Printed "In Memoriam" compositions were fairly common. These were given and kept in the same spirit as many other nineteenth-century mourning remembrances, such as embroidered or painted scenes and wreathes of wax or hair flowers. Similarly labor-intensive, this impressive construction of ornament is realistically architectural and was built piece by piece out of combination borders. The black, metallic silver, and yellow gold inks are suitably reserved; and recognizable mourning symbols, such as urns and praying cherubs, convey the appropriate solemnity. The Relievo typeface here mimics actual carving on a headstone.

In Loving Memory

OF

JOHN GRADY,

Who died 17th September, 1881,

AGED 16 YEARS:

AND OF

GEORGE GRADY,

Who died 1st April, 1886,

AGED 29 YEARS.

" We'll welcome all Thy sovereign will, for
all that will is love ; and when we know not
what Thou dost, will wait the light above."

JESUS, MEEK AND HUMBLE OF HEART, MAKE MY HEART LIKE UNTO THINE

IN MEMORIAM

OUR LIVES ARE NOT GOVERNED BY BLIND CHANCE, AND WE MUST NOT DOUBT THAT
FOR SOME WISE END WHICH WE KNOW NOT AND ARE NOT EXPECTED TO KNOW, OR EVEN
TO GUESS, ALL THAT HAPPENS TO US IS ORDERED AND SETTLED FOR US BEFOREHAND.

12

Stephensons Grocers

J. H. Prouty, Printer, Albany, New York

**Advertisement
1886**

A charming study in wrongheadedness, this specimen flouts every rule of legibility and logic. The printer has proudly attempted a daring, contemporary composition, evidently using whatever he had around the shop. The ad includes no fewer than eight typefaces—many of which were decades old at the time—and a great deal of ornament that was also of an older, more delicate style than the prevailing fashion of 1886.

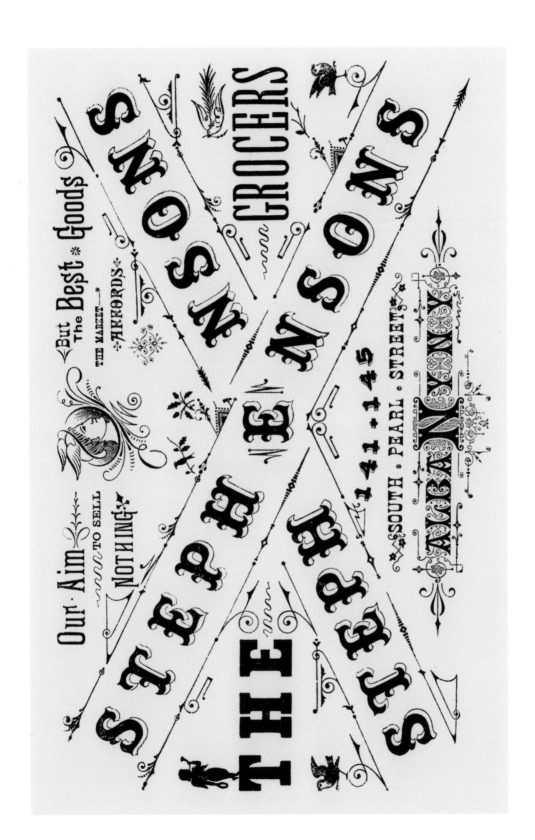

STEPHENSONS
GROCERS
STEPHENSONS
Our Aim TO SELL NOTHING
But The Best Goods THE MARKET AFFORDS
141 145 SOUTH PEARL STREET
ALBANY N.Y.

13

....

**Commemorative
souvenir
1886**

Navy Island Fire Brigade

Ellis, Robertson & Co., St John,
New Brunswick, Canada

This tightly structured and banded composition is essentially a thank-you note from one fire company to another. While the overall effect is attractive—abundant metallic gold, in particular, imparts a certain regal quality—the piece mixes an odd assortment of elements from the extremely refined to the quirkily abstract. Of particular note is the highly ornamented and refined title face, which is paired with a curious outline type called, inexplicably, Santa Claus. The very naturalistic lilies, an aesthetic-movement motif, contrast with the column of starfish-like Santa Claus ornaments.

The Navy Island Fire Brigade

Returns · sincere · thanks · to · the · Members · of

Wellington Hose Company, No. 3

· for · many · Courtesies · extended · while · visiting ·

Halifax · during · the · Firemen's · Tournament ·

✦ August · 10th · to · 12th · A.D. · 1886 · ✦

SECRETARY.

J. F. MORRISON.

J. H. SLATER.

WM. McEVOY.

P. KILLORN.

E. KENNEDY.

WM. ROBSON.

GEO. McGOWAN.

EDW. HANEY.

R. NIXON.

WM. J. HIGGINS.

R. J. WILKINS.

CAPTAIN.

81

14

....

**Circular
1888**

Farmers' and Mechanics' Fair

Charles Gischel, Jr., assisted by George West,
Easton, Pennsylvania

Displaying all of the characteristic compositional eccentricities of George West's office, this design is perhaps even more eclectic than his other specimens. Mixing handmade decorative elements, three families of ornament, and ten different typefaces within a completely subjective division of space, the piece appears completely disordered on first viewing. Closer inspection, however, reveals a certain deliberate and complex balance. The evenness of the printing—extremely fine rules alongside dense darks—shows that it is the product of skilled hands.

Particularly noteworthy are the Combination Silhouette Border (patented 1882), which shows in the child's head and the flowers in the upper left corner, and the drooping brass rules typical of Foster, Roe & Crone's designs.

82

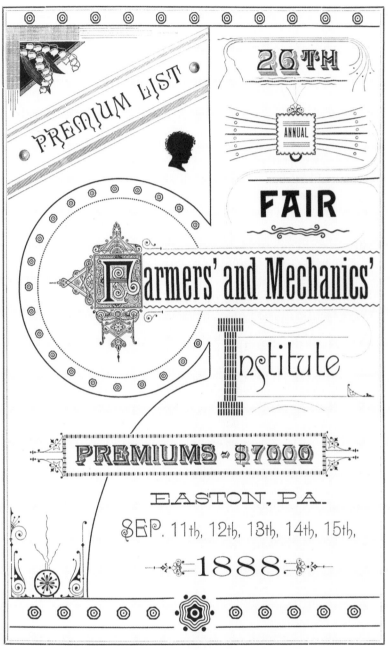

PREMIUM LIST

26TH

ANNUAL

FAIR

Farmers' and Mechanics'

Institute

PREMIUMS ~ $7000

EASTON, PA.

SEP. 11th, 12th, 13th, 14th, 15th,

1888

West's Printing House, Easton, Pa.

CHAS. GISCHEL, JR., ASSISTED BY GEO. W. WEST.

15

Trade card
ca. 1879–81

Franklin Type Foundry

J. F. Earhart, Cincinnati, Ohio

The basic devices of artistic printing—filled corners and banding—are conceived here with appealing graphic immediacy. Minimal text is rendered in two of the most popular typefaces of the period, Glyptic (patented 1878) and the magnificent Relievo No. 2 (patented 1879). The dense corner ornaments are from Zeese and Co. in Chicago.

This particular design was originally created in eight colors by J. F. Earhart for his own trade card. The Franklin Type Foundry liked it so much that they requested that the virtually identical composition be recreated for them, and it is interesting that Earhart saw no problem in acquiescing.

A distinguished printer with especial mastery of color, Earhart went on in 1892 to publish *The Color Printer*, an elaborate and exhaustive "practical guide to ornamental color printing."

Yours truly
John F. Earhart

84

FRANKLIN

ELECTROTYPING.

TYPE FOUNDRY

STEREOTYPING.

CINCINNATI.

16

....

**Trade advertisement
1883**

Parsons, Fletcher & Co.

William J. Taylor, with J. C. Pentney & Co.,
Northumbrian Works, St. Benedict's, Norwich, England

With its oblique band and corner fills, the general composition of this British specimen is similar to that of the Franklin Type Foundry (Specimen 15). On comparison, however, this example is not nearly as balanced or strong. The type—old-fashioned for 1883—is parceled out in white cartouches and reads awkwardly across the divided panel. The piece's most intriguing element is the wide marbled patterning around the edge. Artistic printing is filled with experiments in texture techniques that made use of wood grain, stippling, metal, and even hair. Several similar processes—called variously Chaostype, Metamorphic borders, and Selenotype, among many other names—were developed around the same time. This sample, however, is none of those, and its nature remains a mystery.

86

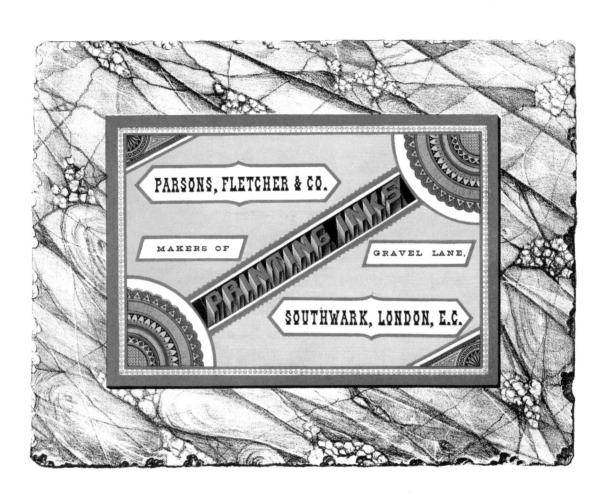

17 Fred Wood, General Printer

Herbert Parker, with Fred Wood, Wexford, Ireland

**Trade card
1885**

The curiously beribboned moon shapes and pendulums seem as though they could be referencing some arcane Masonic symbolism. Most likely, however, they simply illustrate the artistic printer's penchant for creating forms that do not have any direct relation to the subject matter at hand. The curled corners, moons, and banners were created by hand from brass rules and form a display of technical prowess. The *Printers' International Specimen Exchange* marveled at the "typographical talent [shown] in this small office in an out-of-the-way part of the country."

18 George Brown, Compositor

**Trade card
1882**

Whether or not this enigmatic card is American in origin, it would have been considered a bold "American-style" piece as it featured the latest ornament, strong color, and dramatic composition. Strikingly minimalist type holds its own—but just barely—against the strong colors and massive bulwark of ornament. This is also an amusing example of nineteenth-century fastidiousness about punctuation.

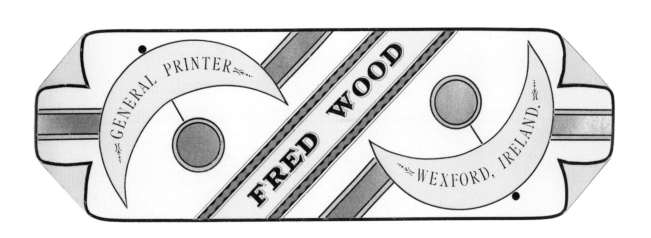

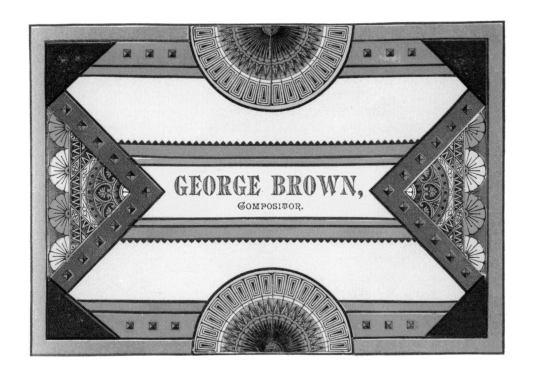

89

19

....

Magazine cover
1887

American Art Printer

Kelly & Bartholomew, New York City

Here is an example of an early cover of one of the
more important journals to cater to the printing trade.
The *American Art Printer*, published by Charles E.
Bartholomew, was one of several magazines that took
the calling of the job printer seriously and sincerely
promoted what was termed the "the art preservative
of all arts." The journal was lively and informal; and,
along with extolling the virtues of fine printing,
dissecting the particulars of job execution, and
discussing the nature of complementary colors, it
imparted such practical tips as how to keep one's hands
smooth.

This design, while dramatically compartmentalized, manages to remain vibrant with its aesthetic-
movement motifs, and the strong title cartouche and
brackets, which have a presciently art deco feel.

The *American Art Printer* changed its cover colors
for each issue, and it completely changed its design
each year.

90

VOL. 1.   July & August, 1887.   NO. 4.

THE · AMERICAN ART · PRINTER

CONTENTS OF THIS NUMBER.

C. E. BARTHOLOMEW,
PROPRIETOR AND PUBLISHER,
22 College Place, New York.

$1.50 A YEAR.   P. S. M. MUNRO, Editor.   25c. A COPY.

20

Trade card
1887

Ernest Hart, Artistic Printer

C. M. Ostrander, compositor, Rochester, New York

The heart with banding featured here is a sweet play on the printer's name. Simply produced in a deep violet on pale yellow background, it has a wonkily asymmetrical arrangement that incorporates several areas of the typically artistic conceit of implied overlapping. The "Chinaman" from the Mackellar, Smiths & Jordan Chinese combination border series adds the requisite exotic touch.

21

Trade
advertisement
1881

Co-operative Printing Society, Printers and Stationers

High Bridge, Newcastle

The vibrant saturated yellow and green, which, to modern eyes, give this British specimen much of its graphic impact, were dismissed in the *Printers' International Specimen Exchange* as "florid." The effective use of Zig-Zag combination-border elements and skewed dragonflies creates a lively visual syncopation. Beautifully balancing the decorative borders are three distinct unornamented typefaces— a chunky sans serif and two condensed serifs— which play with scale and weight.

92

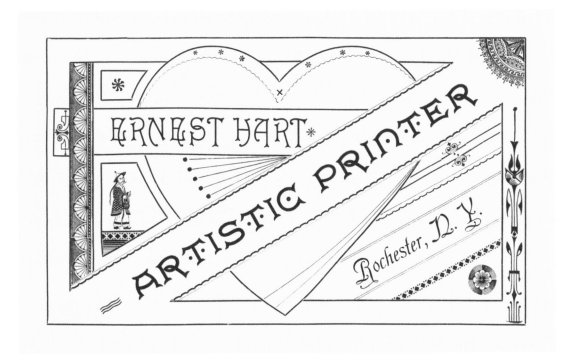

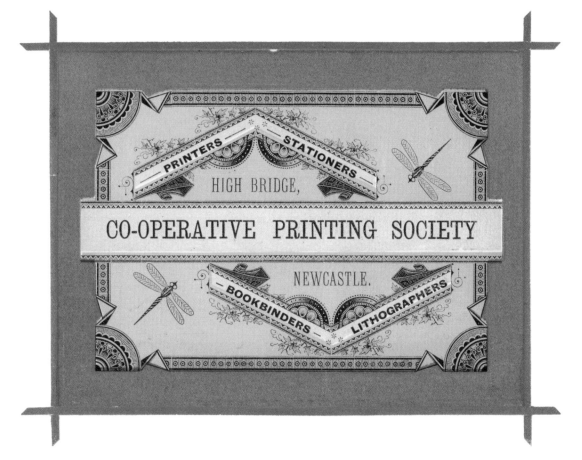

22

Advertisement
1888

Liberty Printing Press

Haight & Dudley, Poughkeepsie, New York

Although the letterpress work is essentially a frame for the engraving of Liberty's new "noiseless press," the quality of this particular frame is outstanding. Hand-curved and "wrinkled" brass rules are intermixed with lengths of ornamental border and flawlessly composed type on curves. The banded and decorated "columns" give the piece a majestic, vaguely Egyptian sensibility. The ad is restrained typographically, with a tightly orchestrated range of pale khaki greens and oranges. The *American Art Printer* called it an "ingenious oddity."

By the time A. V. Haight started his printing business in Poughkeepsie in 1878, he had already exhibited his work to much acclaim. He went on to become a celebrated printer and typographer, and he is credited with the design of several typefaces, including Vassar (1887), Rogers, and Haight (both 1903), as well as typographic ornaments. In 1888, the *American Art Printer* called Haight "indisputably one of the master minds and master hands of American typographic art."

94

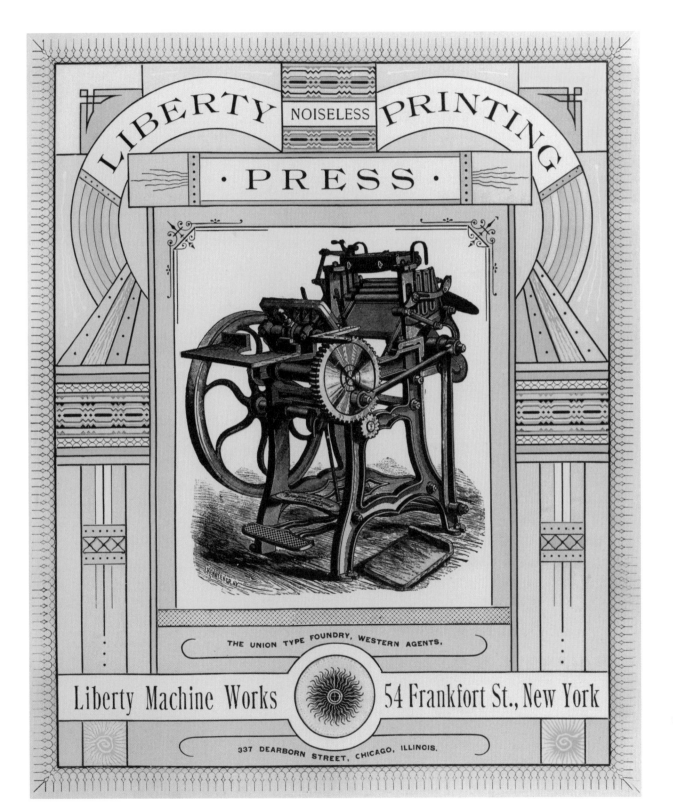

95

23

Calendar for 1883

J. C. Pentney & Co., Northumbrian Works, St. Benedict's, Norwich, England

The variety of elements on this ever-so-slightly disturbing cover is typical of British artistic printing. Typefaces and ornament, perhaps decades old, are mixed with the latest-issue corner fills and borders. An engraving of Father Christmas hovers above a swampy, aesthetic shoreline populated by cranes. Vines curl around the scene in an old-fashioned border, while other foliage intrudes in side branches and a spider-like hanging planter. Competing arcs— the over-scaled, colorful corner fills and the arch of eccentric type—dominate the composition and provide needed weight and color.

96

CALENDAR · FOR · 1883

WITH

Tomlinson and Bromley's

Compliments.

24

**Bill head
1880s**

Butler & Kelley

Butler & Kelley printing, New York City

The popularity of the typeface Relievo No. 2 ("Butler & Kelley") demonstrates just how highly artistic printing valued illusionistic effects, even at the expense of delicacy. Here the darkness of the typeface is perfect for holding the center of multiple borders in black, fawn, and metallic gold. This example appeared in a specimen-exchange volume, but it was probably actually used as a bill head. The firm had its offices on Fulton Street in downtown Manhattan, which, along with the narrow surrounding streets, was the heart of New York's printing district in the nineteenth century.

25

**Bill head
1887**

M. Crane, Electrotyper and Stereotyper

Alfred Butcher of R. W. Lapper & Co., New York City

Electrotyping was a very popular method of reproducing complex compositions, as well as individual types, ornaments, and illustrations and was an improvement over the earlier, nearly ubiquitous stereotype (hence, the modern connotation of the word). An original layout, or "lock-up," of type and ornament that was particularly labor-intensive could be copied by an electroplating process and rendered on a single plate. Printers or type foundries could then sell electrotypes of particularly attractive designs, which accounted in part for the spread of artistic motifs.

Oddly, the *American Art Printer* declared that this printer showed "poor taste in the choice of colors." What stands out, rather than color, is the virtuoso illusion of folded corners, curving banners, and depth.

26

Color-printing
example with
instructional diagram
from *The Color Printer*
1892

Earhart and Richardson, Superior Printers

J. F. Earhart, Cincinnati, Ohio

Earhart's absorption in color letterpress printing is evident in this diagram of the colors and combinations thereof that were used to create the finished printed piece. A master of printing minutiae, Earhart illustrates what he termed the "harmony of distant colors" and indicates how the five ink colors combine in thirty-seven different ways.

The single-minded thoroughness of this example—and of his book *The Color Printer* in general—reveals how advanced the efforts of some letterpress printers and designers were. The spread of color lithography, however, ultimately proved such efforts futile.

100

347

Card showing thirty-seven colors produced by six impressions.   The colors were printed in the following

348—KEY FORM OF PLATE 63.

1.—Gold.
2.—Red.
3.—Red on Gold.
4.—Red lines on Gold lines.
5.—Blue.
6.—Blue on Gold.
7.—Blue on Red.
8.—Blue lines on Red lines.
9.—Blue on Red on Gold.
10.—Yellow.
11.—Yellow lines.

12.—Yellow on Gold.
13.—Yellow lines on Gold lines.
14.—Yellow on Red.
15.—Yellow on Red on Gold.
16.—Yellow on Blue.
17.—Yellow on Blue on Gold.
18.—Yellow lines on Blue lines on Gold lines.
19.—Yellow lines on Blue lines on Red lines on Gold lines.

20.—Gray.
21.—Gray lines.
22.—Gray on Gold.
23.—Gray lines on Gold lines.
24.—Gray on Red.
25.—Gray solid on Red lines.
26.—Gray lines on Red lines.
27.—Gray ou Blue.
28.—Gray lines on Blue lines.
29.—Gray on Blue on Gold.
30.—Gray on Blue on Red.

31.—Gray lines on Blue lines on Red lines on Gold lines.
32.—Gray on Yellow.
33.—Gray solid on Yellow lines.
34.—Gray lines on Yellow lines.
35.—Gray on Yellow on Gold.
36.—Gray on Yellow on Blue.
37.—Gray lines on Yellow lines on Red lines on Gold lines

27

....

**Trade ad
1883**

Boston Type Foundry

In old-fashioned trade parlance, the printing office was referred to as the "chapel." This rather lugubrious evocation of one is painstakingly composed of brass rules and pays homage to a printing press that would already have been considered an antique in 1883. Although it was a promotion for a type foundry, this specimen makes explicit how closely interrelated the businesses of type founders and printers were. The vaulted Romanesque arches even proclaim the printing trade's less-than-euphonious motto: "The art preservative of all arts." The composition was extremely difficult, successfully creating perspective, detailed shading, and vignetting with nested circles.

28

Printers' Novelties

Composed by Henry A. Determan, of R. W. Lapper &
Co., New York

Presented together, these three ads, created by
R. W. Lapper for three separate but related businesses,
are an appealing cascade of type containers. They
show off a family of design elements sold by the
Manhattan Type Foundry, called Baker Brass Rule
Ornaments, which came in 335 pieces at a cost of
$6.50—not an insignificant sum at the time. The
foundry declared that these ready-made ornaments "do
away with the mitering of brass rules [and]
consequently save time and labor." Growing
standardization within the printing and type-founding
businesses offered job printers everywhere, no
matter what their skill level, the potential to add a
fillip of artistic design to their work.

104

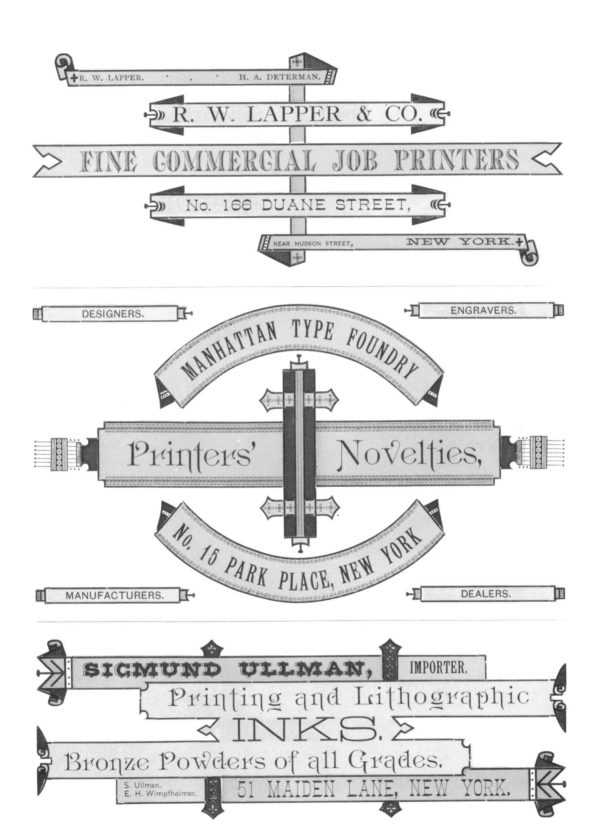

R. W. LAPPER. H. A. DETERMAN.

R. W. LAPPER & CO.

FINE COMMERCIAL JOB PRINTERS

No. 166 DUANE STREET,

NEAR HUDSON STREET, NEW YORK.

DESIGNERS. ENGRAVERS.

MANHATTAN TYPE FOUNDRY

Printers' Novelties,

No. 15 PARK PLACE, NEW YORK

MANUFACTURERS. DEALERS.

SIGMUND ULLMAN, IMPORTER.

Printing and Lithographic INKS.

Bronze Powders of all Grades.

S. Ullman.
E. H. Wimpfheimer. 51 MAIDEN LANE, NEW YORK.

29

Trade card
1891

Louis C. Hesse, Printer

Louis C. Hesse, St. Louis, Missouri

This exquisite specimen manages to parade a variety of shapes and colors in the small space of a printer's business card. Although it is a relatively late piece, the corner-fill and pinwheel decoration are not too far removed from the motifs characteristic of artistic printing. The overall sensibility, however, is far more sophisticated, and all of the ornamental details appear to work in concert. With a minimum of psychological projection, one can see suggestions of movement: paper wrapping a cylinder and gears turning.

106

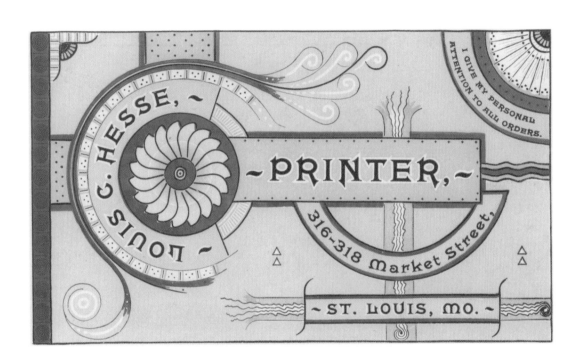

LOUIS C. HESSE, ~

~PRINTER,~

I GIVE MY PERSONAL ATTENTION TO ALL ORDERS.

316~318 Market Street,

~ST. LOUIS, MO.~

30

Trade card
1889

A. S. Prentiss, Printer

A. S. Prentiss, Norwalk, Ohio

Despite the inclusion of a heavy diagonal, which seems like a holdover from an earlier style, this specimen is an intriguing departure from the typical artistic layout. The card's organic, anemone-like forms and tempered colors give it a surreal floating quality. The free-form arrangement and open, sinuous curves seem to point toward the coming art nouveau style. Idiosyncratic curved and "wrinkled" rules were a signature commodity of Foster, Roe & Crone of Chicago and were picked up by a number of printers.

31

**Advertisement
1887**

Bijou Art Emporium

George Seaman, of Haight & Dudley,
Poughkeepsie, New York

Confused and slightly manic, this specimen would
not, by modern standards, be considered a complete
success. Only the use of a single, unornamented
typeface seems to anchor its busyness. The *American
Art Printer*, however, reproduced it, citing its
"admirable restraint" and the effectiveness of its
"simplicity." The magazine was particularly taken
with the fact that "with only six workings"—that is,
six separate passes through the press—and by
making clever use of overlapping tints, the printer
had managed the effect of ten colors.

110

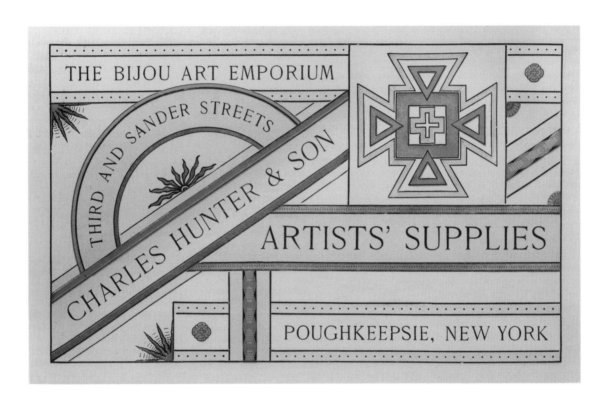

THE BIJOU ART EMPORIUM

THIRD AND SANDER STREETS

CHARLES HUNTER & SON

ARTISTS' SUPPLIES

POUGHKEEPSIE, NEW YORK

111

32

Compliments

Paul E. Werner, Akron, Ohio

Trade promotion
1880

Some observers, such as type historian Herbert Spencer, have noted the latent avant-garde qualities of artistic printing, and this specimen exemplifies the "modern" potential in its methods, elements, and ethos. Sixty years before Raymond Loewy designed the Lucky Strikes cigarette package, Paul Werner, "Superior Printer" from Akron, foreshadows that icon of twentieth-century graphic design.

Five typefaces—some of them fancy—give away the age of this composition, but they maintain a low profile and even weight that don't compete with the spectacular black, red, and metallic gold sunburst surrounding them. The unobtrusive, tan, corner-filled border also reveals a reluctance to relinquish conventional decoration.

112

113

33

**Advertisement
1889**

Los Angeles Printing Co.

Henry W. Kruckeberg, foreman,
Los Angeles, California

It is fairly rare in the specimen exchanges to come across an example from the West Coast. This very attractive and professional ad for a firm in Los Angeles proclaims them to be a "railroad" and "commercial" printer, rather than a "fine" or "art" printer, which means their work likely consisted of schedules, time-tables, charts, and other text-heavy, nonornamental projects. This fact makes the comparatively sophisticated specimen all the more impressive. The reach of artistic printing followed the railroad's push to the Pacific coast, extending new print opportunities along the way, though many of the shops dotted along those rail lines did not have the resources, time, or skill to create artistic specimens.

WM. WRIGHT, Pres.   FRED L. ALLES, Vice-Pres.   C. K. WALRATH, Secy and Treas.

Los Angeles Printing Co.

RAILROAD AND COMMERCIAL **PRINTERS**

231 N. LOS ANGELES ST.

Los Angeles, California.

34

·····················

**Columbus Board
of Trade
excursion brochure
1887**

Beeline

George H. Schenck and Ben Schwartz, compositors,
of T. C. Schenck & Co., Cleveland, Ohio

Shown are the full front and back covers of a
souvenir booklet for the annual excursion of the
Columbus, Ohio, Board of Trade. The cover features
the distinctive scrawled typeface Mikado, here
embellished with a white demi-outline that
exaggerates its already buoyant charm. Prominently
dotted with engraved scenes, the piece's true focus
is on the railroad's realistic namesake.

Although its appearance is scattered, the
brochure combines loose, freehand-looking type and
the natural scenes to impart a rustic charm to the
covers—a visual break from the far more common
Asian influences of artistic printing.

SOUVENIR

* Third Annual Excursion of the

Columbus Board of Trades

TO

Niagara Falls, Saratoga, Lake George, AND THE Adirondacks.

Board of Trade Excursion to Lake George

via

BEE LINE

C·C·C·& I·RY.
I·B·STL·RY.
D·B·U·R·R·

Lake Shore Railway,
New York Central,
AND Hudson Riv. R. R.
AND
Delaware & Hudson
Canal Company.

*Type manufactured by the Thorp M'f'g Co., Cleveland, Ohio.

35

Political flyer
1877

Democratic Ticket

Rockwell & Churchill, Printers, Boston, Massachusetts

William Gaston, the incumbent, lost this election for governor of Massachusetts. His political-party notice is an example of the multitude of the more typical artistic ephemera that did not make it into the pages of a journal or specimen exchange and were preserved by chance. The composition reveals the spirit of artistic printing without relying on trendy aesthetic elements. With the exception of two florettes, the ornament is constructed with brass rules, circles, and triangles—true DIY decoration. The display typeface is Cloister Shaded (1873).

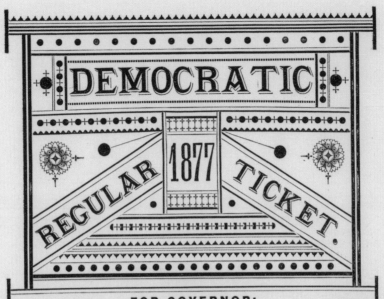

DEMOCRATIC
1877
REGULAR TICKET.

FOR GOVERNOR:
WILLIAM GASTON
OF BOSTON.

FOR LIEUTENANT GOVERNOR,
WILLIAM R. PLUNKETT, ... OF PITTSFIELD.

For Secretary of the Commonwealth,	*For Treasurer and Receiver General.*
WESTON HOWLAND,	**DAVID N. SKILLINGS.**
OF FAIRHAVEN.	OF WINCHESTER,
For Auditor,	*For Attorney General,*
JOHN E. FITZGERALD,	**CHAS. P. THOMPSON,**
OF BOSTON.	OF GLOUCESTER.

For Councillor,
WILLIAM ASPINWALL, ... of Brookline

For County Commissioner,
JAMES M. FREEMAN, ... of Franklin

For Special Commissioners,
ISAAC W. FOLLANSBEE, ... of Medway
ZACHARIAH L. BICKNELL, ... of Weymouth

For Commissioners of Insolvency,
THOMAS E BARRY, ... of Needham
DON G. HILL, ... of Dedham
WILLIAM G. A. PATTEE, ... of Quincy

For District Attorney,
JAMES E. COTTER, ... of Hyde Park

For Sheriff,
AUGUSTUS B. ENDICOTT, ... of Dedham

For Senator,
BUSHROD MORSE, ... of Sharon

For Representative to the General Court,
THOMAS E. BARRY, ... of Needham

36

....

Trade advertisement
1886

Charles W. Fassett, Printer and Stationer

Charles W. Fassett, St. Joseph, Missouri

Combination borders and ornamented type were designed to imitate engraving, in which type and decoration intertwined and overlapped. Here the typeface Arboret (1884) and the Combination Border Series 95 (1884), both from MacKellar, Smiths & Jordan, are used successfully in a controlled design that marshals well-scaled text into numerous containers. The ornament, though slightly funereal, is general enough not to conflict with the subject matter. All is up-to-date, except the extended French Clarendon typeface at the bottom of the composition, which, to the modern viewer, can evoke anything from the Old West to circus posters.

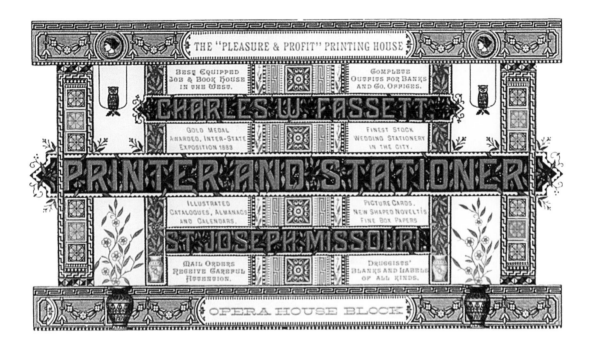

THE "PLEASURE & PROFIT" PRINTING HOUSE

BEST EQUIPPED
JOB & BOOK HOUSE
IN THE WEST.

COMPLETE
OUTFITS FOR BANKS
AND CO. OFFICES.

CHARLES W. FASSETT

GOLD MEDAL
AWARDED, INTER-STATE
EXPOSITION 1888.

FINEST STOCK
WEDDING STATIONERY
IN THE CITY.

PRINTER AND STATIONER

ILLUSTRATED
CATALOGUES, ALMANACS
AND CALENDARS.

PICTURE CARDS.
NEW SHAPED NOVELTIS
FINE BOX PAPERS

ST. JOSEPH, MISSOURI

MAIL ORDERS
RECEIVE CAREFUL
ATTENTION.

DRUGGISTS'
BLANKS AND LABELS
OF ALL KINDS.

OPERA HOUSE BLOCK

37 Moore and Langen, Printers

Moore and Langen, Printers, Terre Haute, Indiana

**Trade card
1885**

Job printers garnered additional business by taking on newspapers and advertising that catered to specific cultural markets. Harpel's *Typograph* and other manuals included sections with typesetting guidelines for Hebrew and German, among other specialties. A town's ethnic concentration would influence where printers got their type and ornament, and ultimately had an impact on the style in which they worked. This elaborately decorated advertisement for German and English book and job printing has a slightly European cast, with its opulent filigree and medievalist touches.

Moore and Langen,

ENGLISH AND GERMAN
BOOK AND JOB

PRINTERS

Nos. 24 & 26 South Fifth Street,
Bet. Main and Ohio Sts.

Terre Haute, Ind.

38

A Guide to Easton, Pennsylvania

George West, Easton, Pennsylvania

....

Book cover (front)
1887

Listed in the *American Printers' Specimen Exchange* as a book cover, this sample may have been a vanity project concocted expressly for submission to the widely distributed annual. This tour de force of peculiarity was created with bent rules, ornamental borders, and tint blocks fashioned around a central, already existing engraving. The cover text reads, "Pleasant Ramble Through and About the Grand Old Town of Easton, Pennsylvainia."

124

PLEASANT RAMBLE THROUGH AND ABOUT THE GRAND OLD TOWN OF EASTON, PA.

THE CIRCLE AND
FOUNTAIN IN
CENTRE SQUARE,

HANDSOMELY ILLUSTRATED!

39

·····································

Book cover (back)
1887

A Guide to Easton, Pennsylvania

George West, Easton, Pennsylvania

This is the back cover of the book-jacket specimen shown on the previous spread. George West manipulated brass rules into the form of a fan and vignetted an existing engraving of a local scene. He has surprinted the colored engraving with several of MacKellar, Smiths & Jordan's silhouetted figural ornaments to surreal effect. West was freely inventive with form and spacing and typically included several whimsical touches in each piece.

A critic at the *American Art Printer* took issue with the colors, calling them "crude and primitive… As they are they give a commonplace look to a meritorious production."

WAGNER'S DAM, ON THE BUSHKILL.

40

....

Trade card
1881

American Model Printer

Kelly & Bartholomew, New York City

Kelly & Bartholomew created this exceptionally lush and articulated trade card for their "sumptuous" self-published journal, the *American Model Printer*. An extravaganza of artistic printing's hallmarks, it manages to employ elaborate layering, angled compartments, corner fills, the illusion of space, ribbons, banners, and an exotic landscape—all in the name of self-promotion. This is artistic exuberance, professionally handled.

41

Peacock Coal

J. F. Earhart, Columbus, Ohio

J. F. Earhart, the consummate colorist, displays a favored peacock-feather motif to illustrate this notice for peacock coal, an iridescent coal variety. An uncommon transparency in the green-and-blue-tinted bands allows the mottled, textured background to show through. While printers regularly overlapped tints, it was primarily in discrete areas and in order to achieve the resulting additional color. Here Earhart seems to be dabbling with Chaostype, his own patented textural process. Created by layering ink printed from plates of random hardened drips of molten metal, Chaostype was, according to Earhart, "suitable for ornamenting all kinds of Fine Book and Job Printing." It became a sensation, and others copied the effect outright or developed variations, calling them Owltype, Selenotype, Cloudtype, and Metamorphic borders.

42

Annual Dinner

David Short, foreman, with John Baxter & Son,
Edinburgh, Scotland

Unusual variations on common shapes—the notched
diamond and nipped central panel—give this dinner
program its interest. Short probably created the
symmetrical, curled linear decorations by bending
brass rules by hand. Although three typefaces are used,
their weight and decoration do not conflict with the
overall elegance.

The printing of metallic colors was called bronze
printing. Fine metallic powders were brushed onto
freshly printed gold or bronze "preparation," an inklike
mixture that provided a wet surface for the powder to
stick to. Once the excess powder was wiped away, the
bronze was allowed to dry, and then other colors could
be surprinted.

132

SEVENTH
ANNUAL DINNER
1887

43

William Holmes & Co. Carriage Repository

Haight & Dudley, Poughkeepsie, New York

Deceptively indifferent-looking, this specimen deftly integrates a surprising array of aesthetic styles: neoclassical ornament, an Ionic column, a Hellenized sphinx, Asian-inspired corner fill, and medieval illumination. The business advertised, a "carriage repository," was probably what we would today call a parking garage.

134

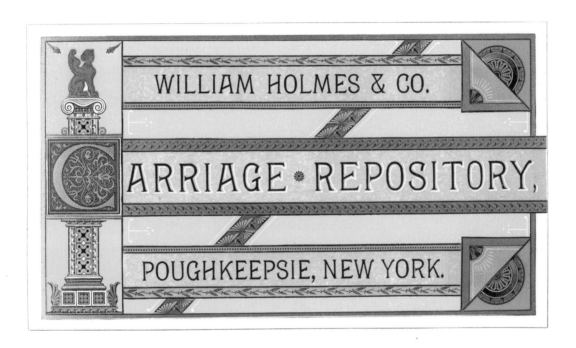

WILLIAM HOLMES & CO.

CARRIAGE • REPOSITORY,

POUGHKEEPSIE, NEW YORK.

44

Dutch Belted Cattle

George West, Easton, Pennsylvania,
with alterations by the *American Art Printer*

**Advertisement
1889**

From the singular vision of George West, this poster mixes three typefaces, bent rules, and an engraving in a very personal interpretation of information and design elements. The eccentricity and highly unusual use of space pushes this specimen into the realm of fine— or folk—art.

The *American Art Printer* reprinted West's poster for instructive purposes, as they did with his embossed bill head (Specimen 51). In what seems like blatant product placement, the magazine specifically calls out West's use of "that most perfect of all rule curvers and twisters, the Earhart Wrinkler." It praises the rule manipulation that created the "Dutch" title, yet the editors apparently felt obliged to add four bits of rule to complete the first letter, "so as to make a perfect 'D.'" Despite its spontaneous look, this specimen's "lesson" was to remind printers of the need to sketch before starting a job.

136

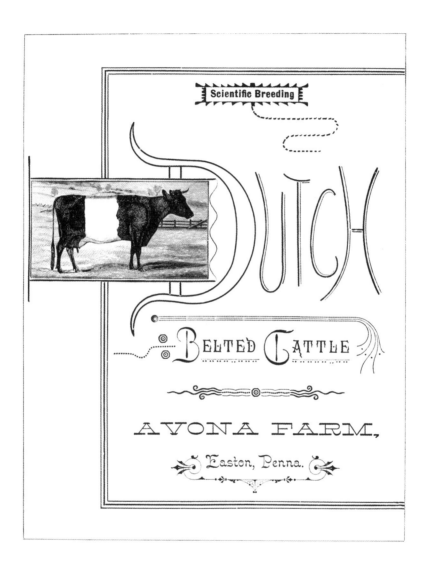

Scientific Breeding

DUTCH

BELTED CATTLE

AVONA FARM,

Easton, Penna.

45

**Trade promotion
ca. 1881**

Kelly & Bartholomew, Printers

Kelly & Bartholomew, New York City

Bartholomew has achieved a complex and unusual balance of elements—offset compartments, multiple banners, and large sunflowers proclaiming the firm's awards at major international exhibitions in Melbourne, Australia, and Paris. Tying it all together is a serene and refined "artistic" color palette. Greens, blues, and yellows—sometimes of indistinct definition—were so prevalent in aesthetic decor, design, and dress that it was commonly parodied. In Gilbert and Sullivan's *Patience*, the posturing aesthete, Bunthorne, frequents fashionable haunts of the day and is described as that "Greenery-yallery, Grosvenor Gallery, Foot-in-the-grave young man."

46

**Anouncement
1884**

Flower Show

H. G. L. Barton, of Barton, Magee & Co.,
Melbourne, Australia

After the 1876 Centennial Exposition in Philadelphia, American type foundry MacKellar, Smiths & Jordan acquired a sales agent in Australia, and the agent's success is evident in this specimen. Broad bands of patterning from the Japanese combination border (1879) wrap the corners, and alliterative phrases fill MacKellar's Zig-Zag border (1880). A large size of MacKellar's gossamer-thin Spencerian Script (1878) announces the flower show—a choice that, while appropriate for the subject, is so delicate it is virtually overwhelmed by the ornament.

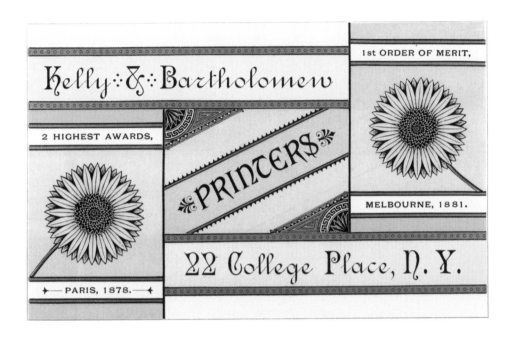

47

Carrier's address
1884

The Press

The Press job shop, Ellenville, New York

Like Greeting! (Specimen 1), this example is a carrier's address. The two pieces could not be more different in design, however. Jaunty bent-rule curls, exclamation points, and a top peak lend the address an impish charm, while the unusual colors and the attempt at interlocking curves hint at more sophisticated ambitions. Made in Ellenville, New York, the birthplace of noted printer A. V. Haight, this piece may have been produced by Haight's own office, although the execution is fairly crude and not up to his usual finish.

The carrier, Ira W. Bailey, who may have been the printer's apprentice as well, is clearly named on the cover, reinforcing the personal touch. The poem inside addressed events of the past year in Ellenville, the nation, and the world.

140

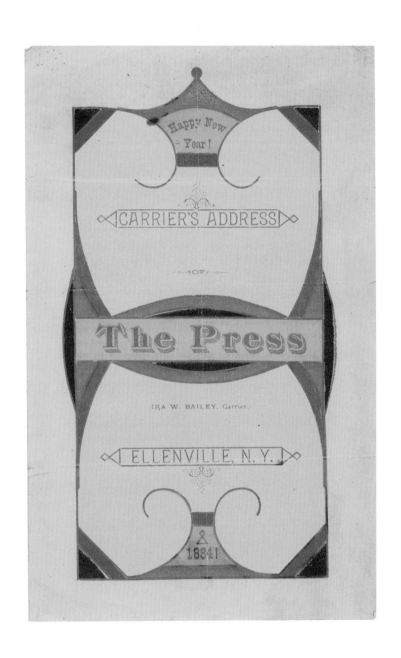

Happy New Year!

CARRIER'S ADDRESS

OF

The Press

IRA W. BAILEY, Carrier.

ELLENVILLE, N. Y.

1884!

48 *Milwaukee Sentinel*

Milwaukee Sentinel job shop,
Milwaukee, Wisconsin

**Carrier's address
1880**

This piece makes extravagant use of MacKellar,
Smiths & Jordan's newly fashionable Combination
Japanese Ornaments series (patented 1879). The
ornaments, employed here with a less-than-exacting
vision of nature, create a dreamily surreal vista,
viewed as if from a balcony. A potted plant sits atop an
ill-considered and mysterious shelf, and puzzling stairs
to nowhere fill the foreground. All is topped off with
a high, swinging bird. Ingenious overlapping of tints
creates the illusion of lavish color, when in fact the
sample was printed from a combination of just three
colors plus black.

In all likelihood the printer intended to illustrate
the four-part poem inside, titled "Life—The Year."
Part III contains two lines that read, "The dawn buds
like an opening flow'r / Slow in the east, soft pink
and gold."

143

49

John Baxter & Son, Artistic Printers

John Baxter & Son, Edinburgh, N.B. (Scotland)

Considering that there is a good deal going on here—bands of titling, intricate compartments of ornament, a floating address ribbon, and, finally, an unusually realistic exotic scene—this specimen is fairly stolid and static. Largely conceived as a complicated frame resembling a shoji screen that parts to reveal a central vista, the design has no direct relation to the subject of printing. Of course, the subtext is that this intricate scene is an example of Baxter & Son's exacting skill and artistic sensibilities. Of technical note is the layering of overprinted color that gives a shimmer to the water and a deep purple cast to the mountain. This entirely plausible landscape, with its fan-wielding figure, contrasts with the somewhat more naïve version in Specimen 48, constructed of the same scenic ornament set issued by the MacKellar, Smiths & Jordan type foundry in Philadelphia.

144

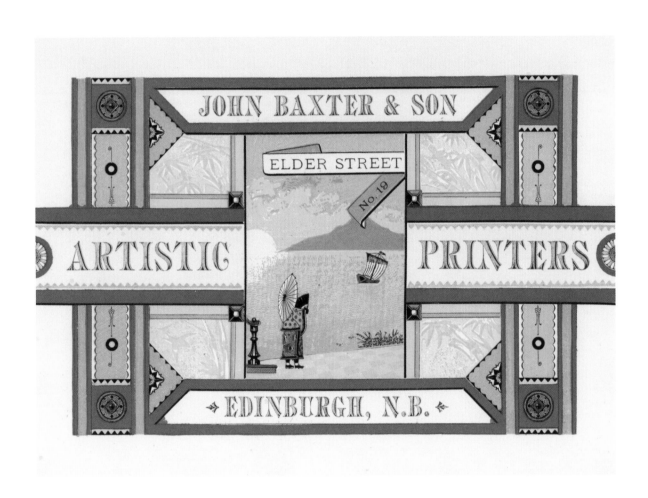

JOHN BAXTER & SON

ELDER STREET

No. 19

ARTISTIC

PRINTERS

EDINBURGH, N.B.

50

Cramer, Aikins & Cramer
Artistic Printers

J. S. Bletcher, Milwaukee, Wisconsin

What resembles an artistic hot-air balloon swagged in beadwork is the central attraction of this unusually trim and compact promotion. Composed with an uncommon lightness and delicacy, the piece is bordered in the marbled, textured border called Chaostype. The sophisticated color choices—salmon pink, deep maroon, and cool gray—seem to anticipate a 1920s urbanity.

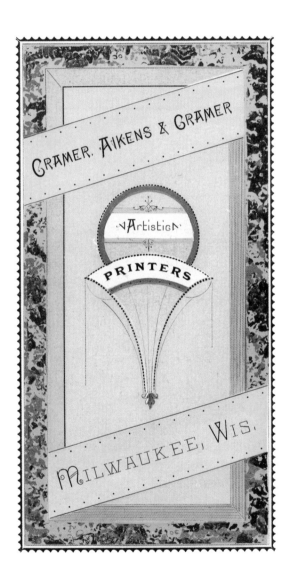

51

**Bill head
1888**

West's Printing House

George West, Easton, Pennsylvania

This playful commercial bill head from George West is extremely labor-intensive, incorporating intricate bent rules, embossing, several colors, and a then-unusual black-and-white halftone image of the printing shop in downtown Easton.

A lavish embossed flourish (not visible in this photo) registers exactly with the descender of the quirky, handmade capital P. At the upper right, West has wittily composed his "Artist Printer" tagline in what is supposed to be a printer's composing stick.

The *American Art Printer* was rapturous, claiming that this specimen showed such "an attractive fresh-ness in design, such unusual adeptness in manipulation, and such exquisite taste and perfect restraint in treat-ment." The magazine reprinted it as exemplary and suggestive of the possibilities available to the artistic printer. It also served as an excuse to plug the Earhart Wrinkler, owned by West and "the most perfect of all rule curvers and twisters."

52

**Trade card
ca. 1879–81**

Eagle Printing House

Haight & Dudley, Poughkeepsie, New York

Haight displays his talent for high-contrast yet complex designs, made up of unique touches. The faceted dog-bone shape features fan-like ornaments, which, instead of filling corners, float in space, each wrapped by a single, elegant curl. The unusually open and airy design offsets an involved pendant crest with a dense "mono-gram" that is actually a layering of all six letters of Haight's name.

Date_____ 188_

WEST'S

PRINTING HOUSE

: GEORGE W. WEST :
:: Artist Printer ::
: EASTON : PENNA :

- PRICES VERY MODERATE -

EASTON·PA.

CHECKS · BRIEFS · PROGRAMS · PAMPHLETS · CIRCULARS · ENVELOPES · DODGERS · POSTERS · CARDS · BOOKS

Mr._____ Dr.

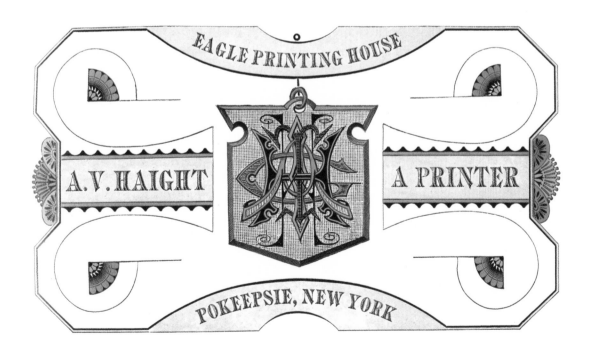

EAGLE PRINTING HOUSE

A. V. HAIGHT   A PRINTER

POKEEPSIE, NEW YORK

53

Advertisement
1882/1888

W. H. Bartholomew & Bro.

William H. Bartholemew and William R. Lambert

Charles Bartholemew, the *American Art Printer*'s publisher, examined and critiqued this ad, produced for his own printing firm and run in the magazine's "Press Room" column. The ad was actually designed in 1882, a full six years before the issue in which it was discussed, an interesting indication that in the nineteenth century, timeliness was a relative matter. The piece was pronounced "very heavy and overdone… with color laid on too coarsely." Bartholomew was particularly harsh about the extravagant use of metallic gold, which he considered "a sheer waste of time and money." It was deemed necessary to remind printers that, while they might be artistically aspiring, they were still businessmen.

150

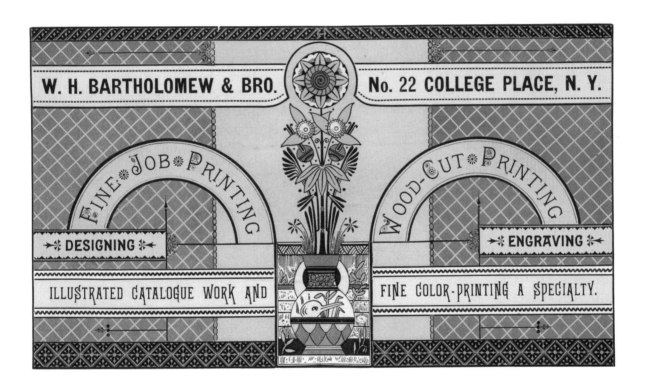

W. H. BARTHOLOMEW & BRO. No. 22 COLLEGE PLACE, N. Y.

FINE · JOB · PRINTING WOOD-CUT · PRINTING

DESIGNING ENGRAVING

ILLUSTRATED CATALOGUE WORK AND FINE COLOR-PRINTING A SPECIALTY.

54

Stark Brothers, Clerical Tailors

John Baxter & Son, Artistic Printers,
Edinburgh, Scotland

With its stripes, pinwheel decoration, and use of the
distinctive French Clarendon typeface, this piece has a
carnival air—not the first thought that comes to mind
at the mention of clerical tailors. The more reserved
left-hand compartment, with its quiet floral ornament
and magisterial crest, seems oddly disengaged from
the full-blown artistic vision with which it competes.

152

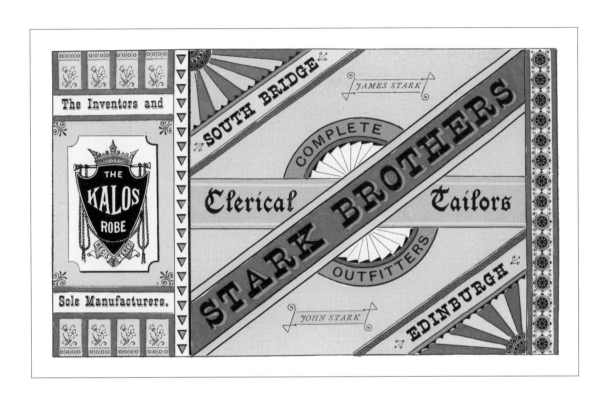

153

55

....
**Advertisement
1887**

Babcock "Optimus" Press

A. J. Smith and John P. Smith, Rochester, New York

Artistic printing at its most outrageous, this specimen is a testament to the individual expression and experimentation that characterized commercial letterpress printing of the period. This kind of freewheeling composition would most certainly have been considered an embarrassing travesty by any number of twentieth-century critics (and was not especially well received by nineteenth-century critics, either). It was examples like these that led to the entire period being dismissed from design history.

The piece's dominant octopoid shape incorporates the illusion of curled paper and seems to carry a diminutive engraving of the featured product—the "Optimus" printing press—in an internal cavity. The pod, created by hand from brass rules, extends swooping lines and radiating tentacles, which display secondary information. Starbursts, piston-like ornaments, and banding that is vaguely reminiscent of conveyor belts give the piece an air of charged animation—and completely overpower its supposed purpose.

154

THE BABCOCK PRINTING PRESS MF'G COMPANY

Barnhart Bros. & Spindler,
Gen'l Western Agents,
CHICAGO, ILL.

NEW YORK OFFICE,
26 and 27
TRIBUNE BUILDING.

Two-Revolution. Lithographic

Drum Cylinder. Stop Cylinder

"OPTIMUS" Two-Revolution Press.

CHAS. B. MAXSON
PRES.
NATHAN BABCOCK
SEC'Y AND TREAS.
GEO. P. FENNER,
SUPT.

NEW LONDON, CONN.

155

56

Trade card
1882

A.V. Haight, Printer

Haight & Dudley, Poughkeepsie, New York

The *Printers' International Specimen Exchange* referred to A. V. Haight as a "versatile prince of printers." He was an accomplished typographer who had an uncommonly refined sensibility and a light touch in composition. Here he restricts himself to one typeface, Eastlake (1879), complementing its light angularity with delicate rule-work and coloring. The aestheticism of the typeface is carried through in stylized floral motifs, a suggestion of sunflowers, fan shapes, and the overall geometry of the composition.

This piece is just one of many Haight-designed self-promotional trade advertisements that were featured in the specimen exchanges. Examples like this one seem to prefigure art deco styling.

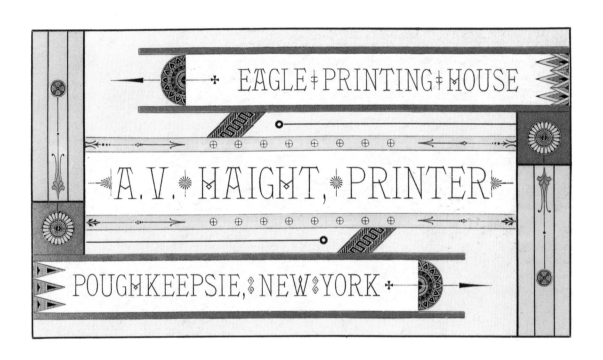

57

Pacific Coast Inventors' Guide

Dwight Germain, of George Spaulding & Co.,
San Francisco, California

Pamphlet cover
1881

The San Francisco firm Dewey & Co. combined patent
soliciting with engraving and publishing and so was
well suited for issuing an "inventors' guide." The
confident artistic style of the specimen and its use of
Japanese ornament at the height of its fashion suggest
that the port of San Francisco was able to respond
quickly to developments in taste on the other side
of the continent.

158

PACIFIC COAST

INVENTORS' GUIDE.

Dewey & Co.

202 Sansome St.

Cor. Pine.

58

Great Remnant Sale

O. F. Thum, with Wayland-Barkley Printing Co.,
Pueblo, Colorado

Specimens like this one from Colorado, so very different in style and level of sophistication than most of the promotional examples collected here, allow a glimpse of the spread of artistic printing to more far-flung markets around the country. As naïve as it is, this piece reveals ambition and apparent skill in its handling of diagonal typesetting, delicate angle fill, and the circular arrangement. The large decorative letters at top may have been wood type and would have been decades old at the time, most likely pre-Civil War.

160

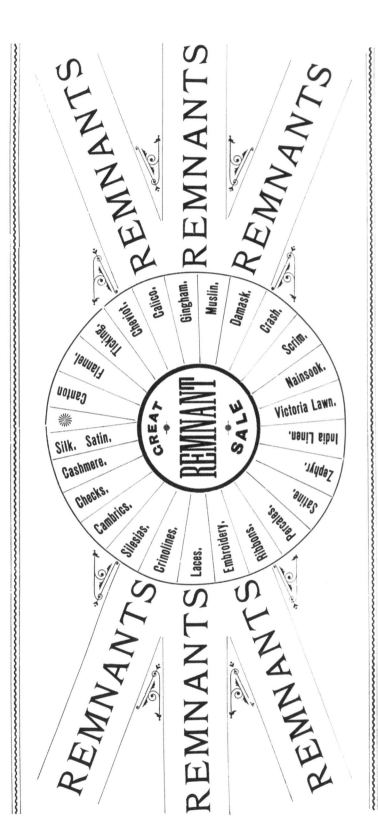

161

59

....

Trade card
1882

John Baxter & Son

George Sutherland, foreman, of John Baxter & Son, Edinburgh, Scotland

The *Printers' International Specimen Exchange* noted that this Scottish designer "appears to be ambitious of emulating American printers in startling design and rich chromatic effects." The specimen's "Americanness"—strong color, bold graphic layout— is quite evident, especially in comparison with more common British samples (see page 31). There are seven colors here—green, pearl gray, yellow, red, gold, light blue, and black—each a separate registration and a separate pass through the press. The *Specimen Exchange* goes on to give a sense of the labor involved in such a piece: "Mr. Sutherland's love of his work and determination to excel are shewn…. [I]n the present instance he made the design, set out the colours, cut the various tint blocks, and executed the presswork— on an old hand-press, at his own home—entirely in the limited hours available from the duties of his position."

60

Trade card

J. F. Sullivan, Wood Engraver

P. S. M. Munro, artist, New York

Despite the fact that the laws of perspective are flung to the wind and the continuity of rules and ornament betrays some technical problems, this is a fascinating composition that resembles an M. C. Escher maze. Completely in the typographic spirit of his time, the printer has rallied eight different typefaces into use, piling up involuted type containers into a magnificent spectacle. The faces include the popular Relievo No. 2, as well as Italic Copperplate in "New York" (patented 1878). The heavy gold and black ornament was sold with Relievo No. 2.

It is worth noting that Mr. Sullivan called himself a "designer," while the printer designates himself an "artist." Oddly, Sullivan does not actually display any of his work in this piece; all of the type and ornament are of metal rather than wood.

164

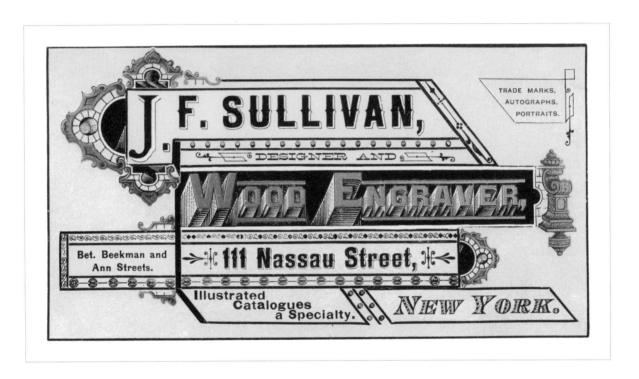

J. F. SULLIVAN,

DESIGNER AND

WOOD ENGRAVER.

TRADE MARKS,
AUTOGRAPHS,
PORTRAITS.

Bet. Beekman and
Ann Streets.

111 Nassau Street,

Illustrated
Catalogues
a Specialty.

NEW YORK.

CHAPTER 3

"Quite Too Awful"

Throughout the period of artistic printing, printers' trade journals and the specimen exchanges cautioned against the excessive use of ornament and counseled regarding the choice of "correct" decoration. In 1887, the eighth *Printers' International Specimen Exchange* noted that perusal of its submissions revealed that "designs that are offensive to good taste and incongruous in ornamentation are…sufficiently numerous to call for protest."[1]

A year later, the *American Art Printer* advised: "Be sure that in the matter of form, everything shall be in keeping. Avoid the distortion of relative proportions or you will unconsciously drift into an overuse or wild misuse of ornament, and consequently into some bizarrerie of coloring."[2] Despite their reservations, however, the authorities never gave up ornament altogether, and the manipulation of liberal amounts of ornament remained a defining characteristic of artistic printing. Hope remained for the discovery of tasteful congruities, and heavily ornamented print design continued into the 1890s.

Graphic design at the end of the nineteenth century followed three paths: it turned to art nouveau, became "historical," or persisted in being "artistic." Despite the popularity of William Morris's medievalism and of the Vienna secessionism's colorful geometries, the use of ornament of any kind in print design faced reappraisal. Asian-style and exotic ornament faded away, except in some art nouveau work, which never found widespread expression in British and American graphic

The underlying rationale for combining ornament in specimens such as this (opposite), published in 1881 in Peter Parley, Jr.'s, *Bright and Happy Homes: A Household Guide and Companion*, came into question in the 1890s.

167

above: **Figure 75**
**Antique-style ornament, by
Field & Tuer, The Leadenhall Press,
London, 1885**
Old- or antique-style printing
featured "primitive" woodcut-type
ornaments that evoked early
letterpress examples.

below: **Figure 76**
**Caslon, created in the early 1700s,
reissued in the 1800s**
Revered by historicists for its
balanced, unadorned legibility,
Caslon remains a popular typeface
today. It is available in several
digital "cuts."

printing ended; the *American Printers' Specimen Exchange* stopped, for example, because of a shortage of submissions.[3] During the 1890s, printing-trade journals lost some of their proselytizing zeal and turned to showcasing anodyne halftone photographs of children, attractive young ladies, and pets. The number of fantastic, multicolored specimens of artistic printing declined. In 1892, the American typefounding industry, source of much artistic ornament, was shaken by the consolidation of twenty-three foundries—that would have been almost every major foundry in the country—into one amalgamation, the American Type Founders Company. While some firms continued independently for a time, specifically advertising that they were not party to the great merger, type foundries lost much of their authority as purveyors and disseminators of taste.

During the time of artistic printing's popularity, publishing as a whole had been evolving into a more standardized industry. Advertising in an increasingly crowded marketplace required promotions of high impact and low cost. Business considerations often led printers to adopt stock display conventions, and type treatments, and easily handled incidental ornament. From a simple technological standpoint, delicate curled rules, whisper-thin typefaces, and involved experimentation did not fare well with the faster and higher-capacity steam- and gas-powered presses that catered to the increased commercial demand. (*Figures 81, 82*) In part, America's leadership in printing technology led to artistic printing's obsolescence.

The younger generation of designers, printers, and artists coming to prominence in America at that time appeared to rebel against the established order. Influential American designer and illustrator Will Bradley (1868–1962) was influenced by European art nouveau, while typographically he was drawn to unornamented faces such as Caslon. (*Figure 76*) Although he began his career in a small-town newspaper shop in the 1880s, likely amidst all the

design. Ornament in the historical style had a dark, thick, medieval or antique quality, as if imitating woodcuts. (*Figure 75*) Some of the last typographic combination borders produced depicted eighteenth-century characters or heavy, tightly curled lines that resembled antique metalwork. Typeface design in America had a burst of experimental vigor, first becoming extremely loose and fluid, like scrawled handwriting, then reverting almost completely to revivals of pre-nineteenth-century unornamented typefaces. Typesetting, especially in book design, pulled in on itself with tightened spacing, leaving wider, unadorned margins. (*Figures 77–79, and 85–87*)

With the changes in design came changes in the professional network supporting the industry, and artistic printing lost its advocates. Some of the trade journals that had supported the style and paraded the confections created with rule twisters and wrinklers ceased publication. Specimen exchanges of artistic

Caslon Old Style

DIME Cash 2

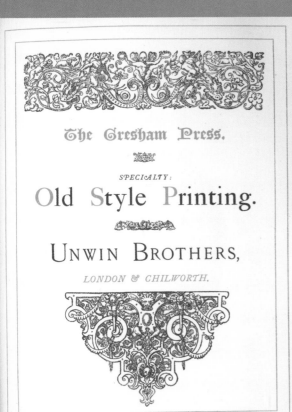

5a 4A, $7.25 — 48-POINT KELMSCOTT — L. C. $2.90; C. $4.35

RELICS OF OLD TIMES
Excellent Styles Revived 28

3a 4A, $5.00 — 36-POINT KELMSCOTT — L. C. $2.45; C. $2.55

COPYING SUPERB PRINTS
Ancient Typography Good 35

10a 5A, $4.30 — 30-POINT KELMSCOTT — L. C. $2.10; C. $2.20

UNIQUE AND HANDSOME LETTERS
Designed by Early Followers of Gutenberg 14

12a 6A, $3.50 — 24-POINT KELMSCOTT — L. C. $1.65; C. $1.85 | 18a 9A, $ — 18-POINT KELMSCOTT — L. C. $1.60; C. $1.60

SUPERIOR MAKE | GOLDEN TYPE FONT
Improved Fonts 60 | Only Kelmscott Press

EDITIONS DE LUXE PUBLISHED MEETING A DEMAND FOR NOVELTIES
Artistic Printing on Uniform Book Lines Old Wine Poured from New Bottles Satisfactory

INLAND TYPE FOUNDRY,
Manufacturers of the Kelmscott Series — 217-219 Pine Street, SAINT LOUIS
STANDARD LINE AND UNIT SETS

THE GOLDING JOBBER.

trappings associated with artistic job printing, Bradley turned his back on the "novelty" typefaces of his youth.[4]

Since the careers of designers like Bradley were built upon their rejection of "Victorian" ornamentation and composition, some of their harshest criticisms of artistic printing correspond with the ends of their working lives, roughly the 1920s through the 1950s. Their early rejections of artistic printing were explained in career retrospectives or in the typographical and printing histories that they were then qualified to write. Meanwhile, the word "Victorian" was fast becoming derogatory shorthand for any and all nineteenth-century decorative excess. Long-simmering dissatisfaction with the eclecticism, experimentation, and supposed pretensions of nineteenth-century graphic design found a culprit in artistic printing. If this generation bothered to acknowledge artistic printing at all, it was with embarrassment. When former printer and librarian-curator of the American Type Founders' Company Henry Lewis Bullen (1857–1938) wrote of nineteenth-century printing in 1922, he admitted, "We now know that our pretty and our startling effects, however well executed, were meretricious to the last degree."[5]

Bullen, older and more steeped in the nineteenth century, was perhaps a little more forgiving of artistic printing than younger designers, who attacked it with startling intensity or tried to forget it ever happened. For instance, in his impressive 1937 study, *Printing Types, Their History, Forms, and Use*, Daniel Berkeley Updike (1860–1941) skipped over the nineteenth century's enormous body of ornamented typefaces entirely, as if they had never existed, and focused instead on the revival of older book typefaces.

In 1944, Clarence Hornung, a prominent commercial artist and editor, wrote unquestioningly:

THE "ARTISTIC" RACE BETWEEN PRINTER AND LITHOGRAPHER CAME AT A TIME WHEN POST [CIVIL] WAR CONDITIONS FAVORED EXTRAVAGANCE AND EXCESSES IN ALL DIRECTIONS, AND NOW MORE THAN EVER, THE TIME APPEARED RIPE FOR THE BOMBASTIC, DISTORTED AND OVER-ORNAMENTAL TYPE FACES AND THEIR PICTORIAL ACCOMPANIMENTS.[6]

Typography historian Frank Denman, in his 1955 book, *The Shaping of Our Alphabet*, titled one chapter

171

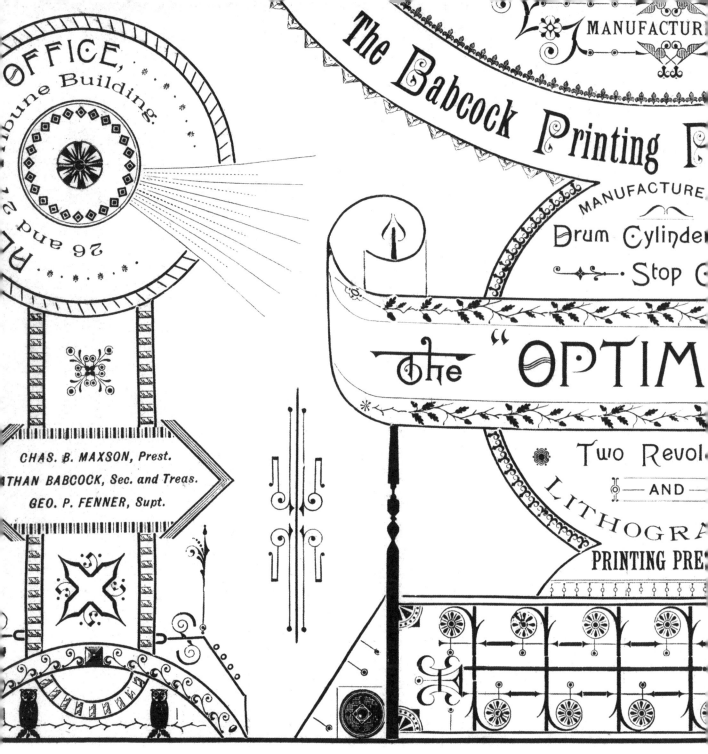

Figure 83
Advertisement for Babcock
"Optimus" Press, 1886

Figure 84
Parlor in the home of Mrs. Leoni,
New York City, 1894

In the parlor and on the page are
two manifestations of the
nineteenth-century penchant
for spatial saturation, eclecticism,
and excess.

"Victorian Confusion: 1850–1890." There he wrote of artistic printing:

> TYPE WAS TORTURED INTO WRETCHED SHAPES AND COVERED WITH GINGERBREAD. IT WAS SET IN TWISTED LINES SURROUNDED BY CURIOUSLY BENT RULES....THE JOB PRINTER TRIED TO MAKE EACH JOB A SPECIMEN SHOWING OFF ALL THE STRANGE FACES HE HAD IN THE SHOP.[7]

In 1944, Andrew Corrigan, looking back on his days as a young printer in the waning years of the previous century, described artistic printing as "quite too awful."[8] His gleeful parody of that nineteenth-century turn of phrase echoes the popular satirical jabs taken at the aesthetic movement.

Corrigan was, in fact, probably the most vituperative critic of late-nineteenth-century printing. His tale of life as a job printer in Ireland, *A Printer and His World*, covers the period from 1896 to the Easter Rebellion in Dublin in 1916. Corrigan attacked artistic printing in language so vivid—so hysterical—that he seemed unconsciously to reveal the very emotional fears that ornament can evoke. For Corrigan, print design during a full three-quarters of the nineteenth century signaled nothing less than "the death of all beauty and life and power…in the craft which enshrined the beauty and power of the written word in all the ages."[9] Corrigan went on to criticize ornamented typefaces and aspects of artistic composition, including the "two cardinal aims of the period: skew setting and filling up space." In a fit of pop-psychological analysis, Corrigan claimed that "the Victorian printer abhorred a vacuum" because it was "an exposure; an uncovering of the compositor's nakedness of invention."[10] With probable allusion to the *horror vacui* of the Victorian bourgeois interior, its every surface an opportunity for embellishment, Corrigan voiced contempt for the filling of every line, whether with type or ornament. (*Figures 83, 84*)

The criticism of ornamented type and design that abounded in the first half of the twentieth century shaped, in part, feelings about ornament in graphic design for the rest of the century. Young designers were not modernists but rather classicists, who turned to the past to help resolve the faults they found with artistic printing. Their work, though conservatively

symmetrical and connected to the past, was in a certain key way like functionalist design: page structure took precedence over ornament. The ornament that did remain was influenced by styles that predated the nineteenth century. (*Figures 85–87*) New decorative styles such as art deco developed during the early twentieth century, but the young designers of the 1890s and their repudiation of artistic printing had a long-lasting, sobering effect on graphic design. Among the first "graphic designers," some college- and art school-educated, that generation looked for new guiding philosophies. Printing instructor Wilbur Fisk Cleaver (1871–1935), who in 1932 criticized nineteenth-century design for its "twisted rules, bird cages and flower pot decorations, all the white space taken up with some decoration," was one of many who identified specifically the source of salvation from the insanity of nineteenth-century type and printing: William Morris, with his Kelmscott Press.[11] The future of print design became "revival."

TURNING TO HISTORY

Wilbur Fisk Cleaver credited William Morris (1834–1896) with instigating a "marvelous change"[12] that virtually saved typography and printing. In doing so, Cleaver articulated a commonly held belief of the early twentieth century that nineteenth-century print design was a chaotic, unprincipled mess. Morris stressed harmonious page design, and favored handwork in all stages of book production. These developments in book design in the 1890s were called a "revival of fine printing," a phrase signifying a return to printing customs that preceded the nineteenth century and implying that everything that had come immediately before was distinctly not "fine." Morris, a well-educated, upper-class professional designer, provided the nascent profession of graphic design with a compelling alternative to artistic printing.

Morris's influence was pervasive. He was a prominent artist, poet, and social activist, as well as a designer of textiles, wallpaper, and, of course, the printed page. He became a model for the artist-printer, an individual unfettered by popular taste and dedicated to a personal vision, guided by strongly held beliefs. His romantic

STUDLEY

Arlington Oldstyle

medievalism and utopian poetry were enlivened by radical socialism, stubbornness, and a fierce opposition to the politics and economics of his time. He was a social reformer dedicated to improving life in all ways, but especially through the creation of more attractive and rational homes. He hated the elitist overtones of aestheticism, although his lushly patterned wallpapers and textiles, his color palette, and even his tall, dark-haired wife came to be recognized as some of the best-known symbols of that very movement. [13] Renowned for his fits of temper, Morris was a passionate, impatient, imposing, messy force of nature.

Strongly influenced by art critic and social theorist John Ruskin (1819–1900), Morris reveled in all forms of the Gothic, from its intricate, decorated manuscripts to its lofty cathedrals. He and a coterie of like-minded friends despised the High Renaissance, the politics it represented, and especially what they saw as the pompous theatricality of the painter Raphael (1483–1520) and his circle. No matter how tastes around him shifted, the pre-Renaissance represented to Morris—and to his self-proclaimed "Pre-Raphaelite" artist friends like Edward Burne-Jones (1833–1898)—a time when individuals made meaningful contributions to society through craft. Morris's historicism found a moral base in the idealized past. From its first book, the Kelmscott Press was extremely influential, especially in America and Germany. [14] However, Morris's influence on questions of ornament in particular is complicated. He was a transitional figure who called for reform yet without turning his back on the past and ornament, as he was very fond of dense, interlaced borders and adorned initial letters. (*Figure 88*) Essentially, Morris offered yet another alternative to the stylistically eclectic period. He did it with such force of character, though, such moral authority, that, even when printers

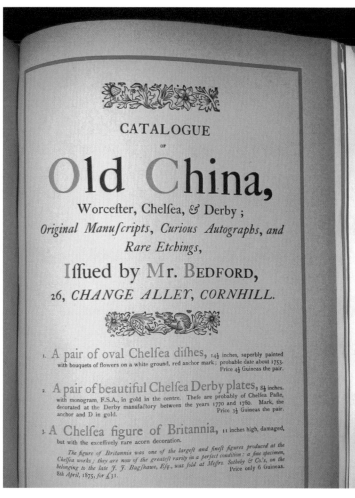

top, left: **Figure 85**
Studley, advertisement detail, ca. late 1890s

top, right: **Figure 86**
Arlington Oldstyle, ca. 1898

Antique-style ornament and plain or revival-style type remained commercially popular well into the twentieth century.

above: **Figure 87**
Catalogue of Old China,
published by Field & Tuer, the Leadenhall Press (1881)
Historicist print reformers went so far as to use deliberately antiquated spelling and characters. The *Printers' International Specimen Exchange* referred to "ye Leadenhall Presse" as a band of "Merrie Menne."

175

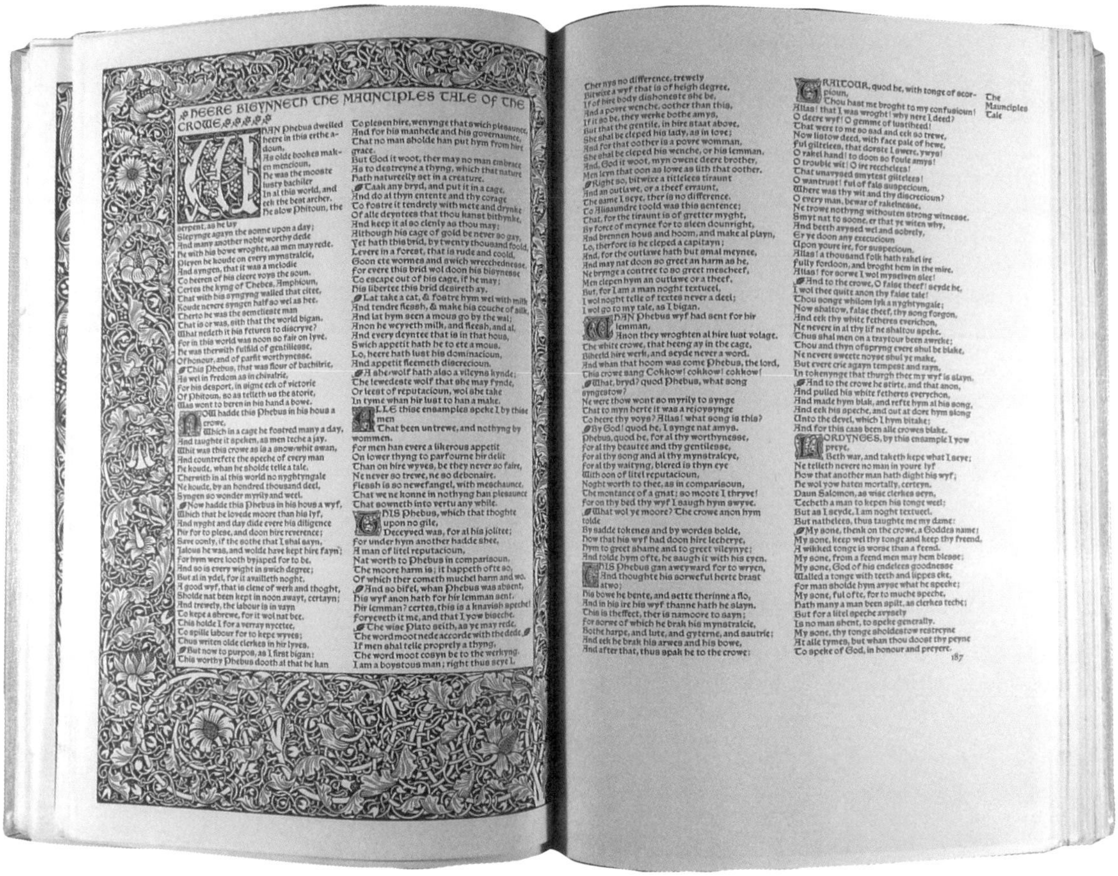

Figure 88
The Works of Geoffrey Chaucer,
**published by William Morris
(1896)**
Although Morris and his dense
medievalist vision cannot
be credited with taming the
nineteenth-century penchant for
ornamental display, his work did
signal a change in print design
and ended the enthusiasm for
Asian exoticism.

and designers could not apply his medievalism directly
in their work, they found in him a focus for their desire
to execute a decisive change.

Morris's relationship to artistic printing is con-
fusing if thought of in terms of dichotomies such as
handicraft versus machine production, the aesthetic
movement versus arts and crafts, or ornamentation
versus simplicity. Would he support artistic printing as
the creation of individual craftsmen, or condemn it as
industrial manufacturing? And is it ironic that his work
precipitated the end of artistic printing? Morris left
no record of comment on artistic printing per se, but he
was famous for his dislike of machine-made or mass-
produced goods. In 1851, as a young man of seventeen,
for example, he refused to enter the Great Exhibition
of the Works of Industry of All Nations. [15] At the same
time, Morris would likely have found distasteful

many aspects of artistic printing: its enthusiasm for novelty, its class aspirations, uneducated taste, and aesthetic mutability.

Although Morris is credited most highly for galvanizing change in book design and typography, his legacy can more accurately be described as the legitimization of historical typography through the strong, consistent manifestation of vision in materials and design. The impact of his work and of that of his associate, printer and engraver Emery Walker (1851–1933), upon the historical appreciation of type was profound and lasting. Type historian Stanley Morison, writing in 1963, testified that Morris and Walker's enterprise "gave an impetus, still strong, to the practice of calligraphy and typography as decorative arts. Morris and Walker created an era of taste and collecting…and created generations of British and foreign admirers of manuscripts and early printed books."[16] Morison mentioned more specifically the contrast between late-nineteenth-century printing and Morris's great book, the Kelmscott Chaucer. The volume not only challenged a "half a century of exploitation [that had] reduced the mass of printing almost to the level of one of the lowest aspects of ruthless industrialism," but it had also made possible a rise in the status of printing, which "henceforth became once more intimately associated with literature and art." Morison suggested that artistic printing was anything but artistic because it was not associated with pedigreed or artisanal pursuits and was instead mere "industrialism." [17]

Morris's Kelmscott Press fostered an association between antique-style type and methods of production and the concept of good design. Revival typefaces came to symbolize quality and progressiveness in print design. The unornamented eighteenth-century English Caslon became popular for books, as well as for ephemeral printing, to such a degree that the survival, dissemination, and use of the typeface intrigued type historians long into the twentieth century.[18] Caslon had never actually disappeared during the nineteenth century; a few English publishers continued to use it. These publishers—notably the Chiswick Press—earned praise from twentieth-century type historians for their adherence to typographic values. Simultaneous with artistic printing's popularity was another style of job printing called the "old," "antique," or "chapbook" style; it imitated printing practices of the fifteenth century to the eighteenth century. Employing rough paper, few colors, crude-looking typefaces, and deliberately anachronistic spellings, this antique style was more popular in Britain than in America. One of its most prominent exponents was Andrew Tuer's Ye Leadenhall Press. Samples of antique printing, striking in their contrast to the examples of artistic printing, are scattered throughout the pages of the *Printers' International Specimen Exchange*, which Tuer oversaw from 1880 to 1887. In the twentieth century, historic, unornamented typefaces such as Baskerville and Bembo were revived by typographical scholar Stanley Morison, as a consultant to the Monotype Corporation foundry. In his role as typographical consultant to the *Times* of London, Morison also commissioned a new typeface based on one from the sixteenth century. This typeface, Times New Roman, has become so common that it is now, in the twenty-first century, practically the default choice for a digital serif type in word processing.

Historians have been eager to credit Morris with revolutionary influence, and the question arises why the printing world was ready to hand him such authority. The embrace of artistic design by consumers on both sides of the Atlantic and the eagerness of manufacturers to satisfy market demand put design in a precarious position—one vulnerable to criticism of alleged pandering. Printers were ready for any strong voice that combined moral authority with aesthetic talent, whether or not its rationale or proposed forms were completely relevant to their practice. There was enough correspondence between Morris's beliefs and widespread doubts about the integrity and legitimacy of artistic printing and ornament that he could assume the role of savior.

CAPTAIN COSTENTENUS
THE GREEK ALBANIAN

Tattooed from Head to Foot in Chinese Tartary as punishment for engaging in Rebellion against the King.

CHAPTER 4

The Ethics of Ornament

"Degenerate," "meaningless," "barbaric"—these words capture the disgust and disdain artistic printing provoked in critics.[1] These psychologically loaded terms suggest they were not concerned merely with a passing fad or superseded technology. These were moral judgments, triggered not so much by the specifics of artistic printing as by one of its integral components: ornament. The moral interpretation of ornament, in other words, was behind most of the brickbats aimed at artistic printing, and is therefore key to understanding the criticism.

The accumulation of design manifestos and art historical scholarship during the nineteenth and twentieth centuries bequeathed many judgments about ornament to our contemporary attitudes. Still other convictions are based on ancient associations between ornament, expression, and artifice. In the search for appropriate, meaningful design styles in the nineteenth century, for example, the cataloging of international decorative modes by designer Owen Jones, the meaning and value of ornament began to be codified. The nineteenth century's "Battle of the Styles" among advocates of varying historicist approaches to architecture ascribed moral significance to building styles, as well as to their ornamental components. Gothic, for example, was equated with Christianity and expressiveness, while Greek architecture was rational, democratic, pagan, and, to some, "meager."[2] Developments at

In the late 1870s, Captain Costentenus exhibited his heavily tattooed body, the result—he claimed—of punishment he received at the hands of Chinese defenders of the throne. Such self-ornament was judged a sign of unrestrained sensibilities and well into the twentieth century taken to represent the primitive and culturally alien.

the turn of and into the early twentieth century, especially in architecture, left us with some of the harshest assessments of ornament. These critiques radically reinterpreted ornament or rejected it altogether. Though rarely addressed, ornament in graphic design has been subject to the same judgments that buffeted architecture and other decorative arts. Artistic printing suffered in particular: from the ridicule of its expressiveness to the criticism of its imitation of other kinds of printing and dismissal on the grounds of its associations with commerce, mass production, and popular taste.

Ornament is obviously not the only means of expression in design, but it is more suggestive and thus perhaps invites interpretation more easily than other modes of elaboration. Because ornament—whether floriated, geometric, or figural—retains associations with objects and periods distinct from those being ornamented, it appears to offer more information and inevitably reveals something of its creator. For the young designers of the late 1890s, artistic printing revealed both too much and too little. The caprices of printers were well on display, while apparent lapses in judgment or knowledge evidenced a lack of concern for function. Self-expression, curiosity, and playfulness—sources of creativity that had once been celebrated not only by artistic printers but by the aesthetic movement as well—became instead wellsprings of an "inappropriateness" that was incompatible with cultural aspirations. Former printer Andrew Corrigan declared of print design that it is "far too easy to revert from elegance to ugliness merely as a natural

180

assertion of individuality."[3] Paradoxically, he also eulogized the "true craftsman," as an artist "in some personal, individual sense," who could find pride in his design "so long as he might plan and execute it as a form of self-expression, and point it out as his own."[4] Corrigan's apparent self-contradiction reveals some of the ambivalence about printing's status as either an art form or a craft. The only way to make sense of the double standard is to assume that Corrigan supported expressiveness only when it was bounded by traditional standards and styles. Artistic printing was not a free-for-all, though it was often described as such. Most commentary in the journals and specimen exchanges mentions both thoughtfulness and restraint, notions that had subtly differing relationships to ornament. "Thoughtfulness," fitness, appropriateness, harmony, and adherence to principles communicated a careful use of rather than the elimination of ornament. "Restraint," on the other hand, conveyed more judgmental and moralistic.

For many, artistic printing was the ornamentally profligate detritus of the printing tradition, untutored craftsmen wallowing in technological ostentation; it was the opposite of thoughtfulness and provoked deeply ingrained associations between ornament and culture. Historian James Trilling asserts that "restraint is assumed to imply a higher degree of individual or cultural maturity," whereas expressiveness is characteristic of the lower orders.[5] Like children or "primitives" encountered by Western explorers, artistic printers were characterized as dazzled by trinkets and cheap

frippery. Commenting in 1883 on the typography of book titles, *The Art Age* claimed that artistic printers could no more be restrained from overusing ornamental type than a "small girl could be prevented from wearing on all occasions her snaky gilt brooch and huge earrings." Such printers were as deluded about propriety as a "Kickapoo brave…when he paints his face red and yellow" in order to "set off his manly figure."[6] Once the moral correlation is drawn between society and the arts, the corresponding hierarchy among cultures could be extended to design. Design that reflected the foundations of Western culture—its classical beginnings as they survived in the typographic traditions of western Europe—was "higher" than the experimental expressiveness of artistic printing. The proliferation of mass-produced ornament and its use by untrained craftsmen could not be reconciled with conceptions of cultural continuity, especially since printing was thought to be "The Art Preservative of All Arts."[7]

The notion of a hierarchy of cultures pervades nineteenth-century commentary, especially with respect to the presumed divide between the primitive and the civilized, but between Europe and America as well. Whether concerning printing or culture generally, America's "great experiment" in democracy presented an intriguing case study in freedom's effect on design practice. Americans boasted about the liberty of their printer-designers to be more than mere imitators, whereas Europeans distrusted the ability of common craftsmen to create articles of aesthetic value. In the early nineteenth century, French political thinker and

GEO. H. MORRILL & CO.

PRINTING INKS

Figure 89
Advertisement for
George H. Morrill & Co. printing
ink factory, 1891 (detail)

social philosopher Alexis de Tocqueville (1805–1859) criticized the effects of democracy on industrial design. According to him, democracy gave license to the creation en masse of imitations of the accoutrements of aristocratic life. This was folly, he believed, because, while the great quantity of imitations raised standards of living, their production was compromised by the expediency of their manufacture. The benefits were undermined by what historian Marvin Fisher identified as a concomitant "loss of utility, aesthetic meaning, and even morality."[8] This pessimistic view placed little faith in the ability of technology and education to progress without privileged oversight, and it advocated the restriction of the means of artistic production to craftsmen who understood tradition and met with the approval of patrician tastemakers.[9]

Burgeoning technologies and the inability of designers to maintain control had been cited as one of the specific failings of the designs featured in the Great Exhibition of 1851 and as a primary concern of nineteenth-century aesthetics in general. For example, the German architect and historian Gottfried Semper (1803–1879) wrote, on the closing of the Great Exhibition in 1852, that an "abundance of means"—new manufacturing processes and rampant industrialization—and the inability of artists to marshal them appropriately posed the greatest challenge to art.[10] (*Figure 89*) Within the printing world, editors of the 1887 *Printers' International Specimen Exchange* noted that the improvements in the printing trade that had taken place during the previous decades constituted a "revolution" in the business but that it was "questionable if the workman has kept pace with these improvements in his training, practical knowledge, or tastes." The writers contrasted the printers' use of ornament in the past, when it was scarce, often hand-made, and judiciously employed, with the "endless profusion" of it in the present, which led to designs that were "offensive to good taste and incongruous in ornamentation."

Concerns about "bad" design were heightened by the implications of mass production. Mistakes or lapses in taste would be multiplied and broadly disseminated; that a proliferation in quantity would result in diminish-

ment of quality seemed irrefutable. The rise of individual choice in the design and selection of products—a natural outgrowth of the proliferation of goods, as well as an extension of the aesthetic movement's emphasis on the individual—revealed the supposed deficiencies in popular taste. Historian Linda Dowling has called the mass-produced decorative arts of the nineteenth century the "democratic" arts and declared that they were a blight on the landscape.[11] The discerning eye could not rest; everywhere it looked it was beset by "cut-rate chromolithographs, banal suburban villas, clothing and carpets shrieking with aniline dyes, an urban wilderness of advertising placards." To this inventory we can add artistic printing. In 1884, *The Art Age* bemoaned the widespread belief among editors that "popular art is inconsistent with simplicity."[12] Artistic printing was "democratic" both in its creation and in its consumption, because much of it was essentially ephemera made for mass consumption. It was the product of tradesmen experimenting with style—often with the latest technical gadgetry—acceding to the demands of the public. It was therefore perceived as frighteningly insubstantial, unmoored from meaning, adrift without antecedent, fleetingly pleasing, seductive, even infectious for undiscriminating consumers. A source of the judgment against artistic printing was the broader mistrust of consumers, the masses who, if given the chance, would commandeer design and send it hurtling toward an ignominious demise.

The decline of artistic printing was a thinly veiled criticism of popular taste and expression, at the heart of which was an aversion to ornament that came to pervade all the decorative arts and that increased in the twentieth century. Commentary on ornament in the early twentieth century, when eclecticism still held some influence in the decorative arts, was particularly biting. Following the disastrous brutality of World War I, many young Europeans found nineteenth-century excesses and eclecticism meaningless. In *A Cultural History of the Modern Age*, historian Egon Friedell described the typical turn-of-the-century Viennese bourgeois home:

THE MORE TWISTS AND SCROLLS AND ARABESQUES THERE WERE IN THE DESIGNS, THE LOUDER AND CRUDER THE COLOR, THE GREATER THE SUCCESS. IN THIS

183

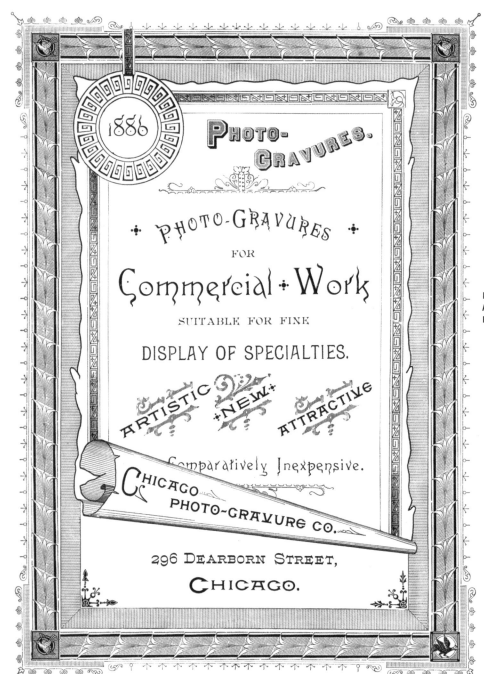

Figure 90
Advertisement for the Chicago
Photo-Gravure Co., 1886

CONNECTION, THERE WAS A CONSPICUOUS ABSENCE OF ANY IDEA OF USEFULNESS OR PURPOSE; IT WAS ALL PURELY FOR SHOW.[13]

It was into this environment, in 1908, that Viennese architect, theorist, and author Adolph Loos (1870–1933) launched the best-known attack on ornament, "Ornament and Crime."[14] By this time, ornament had been separated from meaning and value. "Ornament is no longer organically linked with our culture," Loos declared. "It is no longer the expression of our culture."[15] When ornament ceased to connect with any real meaning, it became extraneous. Its only role was concealment. Many of the diatribes against artistic printing and against Victorian design in general used words such as "false," "fake," and "sham." In 1936, for example, historian Nikolaus Pevsner wrote of the 1851 Great Exhibition in London:

IT IS SUFFICIENT TO SAY THAT MANUFACTURERS WERE, BY MEANS OF NEW MACHINERY, ENABLED TO TURN OUT THOUSANDS OF CHEAP ARTICLES IN THE SAME TIME AND AT THE SAME COST AS WERE FORMERLY REQUIRED FOR THE PRODUCTION OF ONE WELL-MADE OBJECT. SHAM MATERIALS AND SHAM TECHNIQUES WERE DOMINANT ALL THROUGH INDUSTRY.[16]

Pevsner was echoing design reformers contemporary with the Great Exhibition, who found fault with the encrusted ornamentation of carpets, ceramics, wallpapers, and other objects on display—most of which was a slavish imitation of natural form.[17] Artistic printing's transgression was its imitation of other crafts, such as engraving and lithography, and their compositions, colors, and typography. Technological innovations made possible debased imitations of lithography and supposedly led artistic printers away from the acknowledged foundations of conventional printing.

According to its critics, artistic printing even obscured its reason for being. A letter in the *American Art Printer* expressed the fear that the style neglected its typographic messages by placing too much emphasis on ornament, *(Figure 90)* and "instead of the text being

made the basis of the structure, the essence of the job, it now becomes of very small importance indeed—a mere matter of detail."[18] Twentieth-century type historian Herbert Spencer astutely noted the avant-garde qualities of artistic printing's composition but found that,

THE POTENTIALITIES OF THIS DEVELOPMENT WERE OBSCURED BY THE ELABORATE ORNAMENT AND DECORATION—OFTEN QUITE UNRELATED TO THE SUBJECT MATTER OF THE TEXT—IN WHICH [ARTISTIC PRINTERS] SHROUDED THEIR PRINTED ANNOUNCEMENTS.[19]

Shrouding, obscurity, concealment: Ornament was fast acquiring seamier connotations. A significant fear prompted by artifice—and therefore by ornament—was that it also had the potential to be mere gilding on a rotten core. Artifice, ornament, and the "freaks" of design were more than irrelevant or passé; they signaled a pathology. The encrustation of ornament threatened to calcify culture, to hold back progress. It was one of the insalubrious aspects of nineteenth-century life that needed to be eliminated. In the twentieth century, Loos declared that the "ornament disease…is a phenomenon either of backwardness or degeneration."[20]

DEFORMITY and CONTAMINATION

Condemnation of artistic printing captured on the small stage some of the larger preoccupations of the turn of the twentieth century: diffuse anxieties about cultural and societal dilution. In America especially, a country in the midst of waves of immigration, industrialization, and mounting commercialism, fear of chaos and disintegration lay behind at least some of the more shrill condemnations of the practice. Social reformers concerned themselves with the eradication of infectious disease; the rehabilitation of slums, even, at the extreme, with societal purification and the eugenics movement. Artistic printing's profusion of typefaces and its commingling of ornamental elements of disparate reference appeared to hint at a cultural attenuation. If artistic printing was rooted in personal expression,

Mischievous and Destructive

FIGURE 91. ORNAMENTED NO. 1566, ca. 1894

PRIZE·FIGHTS ~PRESS·APPLE~

FIGURE 92. OWL, ca. 1885

DISCARDED·WRITINGS

FIGURE 93. STIPPLE, 1890

Conceits of Modern Design

FIGURE 94. ALPINE, ca. 1885

DANGER

FIGURE 95. MODOC, 1884

Something New Each Day

FIGURE 96. MIKADO, ca. 1886

Flower

FIGURE 97. MATHILDE, ca. 1888

Freak Series.

PATENT APPLIED FOR.

FIGURE 98. FREAK, ca. 1889

⤞TRINAL⤝
SERIES ONE.

SERVICE REFORM 34

FIGURE 99. TRINAL, 1888

then there were no rules: all form, no matter how
distorted, was potentially valid, and print design could
descend into a bedlam populated by "freaks." For critics,
the intemperate use of ornament threatened to invade
and overwhelm the clean certainties that should govern
design. How far could such liberties be taken? When
was beauty achieved? What would be left in the way
of standards?

Ornament was symbolically potent and potentially
threatening. Its fundamentally transformative nature
could make wood look like marble and marble like a
bouquet of flowers. Be it carved embellishment on a
piece of furniture or trompe l'oeil pins in an advertisement, ornament was especially vulnerable to criticism
because much of it was intent on creating an illusion.[21] *(Figures 100, 101)* It was, however, the design of
ornamented typefaces, a mainstay of job printing, that
inspired the most revulsion. Unconventional versions
of traditional letterforms, ornamented types, by design,
were transformed for no practical purpose.

Following the first wave of fancy typefaces issued
in the 1870s and '80s, metal type experienced a second
burst of experimental fervor. Going beyond mere ornamentation, these faces were mannerist exaggerations
that bore extra appendages or sprouted barbs, tendrils
or other accretions, in the manner of hybrid or grafted
plants. This strain of typeface ranged from jagged,
almost electrified forms to loose scrawl. There was even
one called "Freak." *(Figure 98)* In the pages of the noted
journal *The Inland Printer,* such faces were described as
"grotesque mongrel-shaped specimens."[22]

The parts of individual pieces of type are named
in terms of human anatomy: face, head, foot, etc.
Andrew Corrigan extended the analogy to human
pathology. In describing lithographers, who reputedly
violated typography, he wrote that they:

COMMITTED EVERY ABORTION BUT THE ONE WHICH
WOULD HAVE BEEN WELCOMED; THEY PERPETRATED
EVERY MUTILATION BUT STERILITY. THE DEGENERATES
SWELLED AND PULLULATED, FARROWED THEIR LITTERS
AND SPAWNED THEIR MONSTROUS SHOALS UNTIL THE
WORLD OF CASLON AND BASKERVILLE, JENSON AND
BODONI AND ALDUS, BECAME THE WORLD OF CALIBAN,
THE HOME OF A BASTARD BROOD WITH THE BLOOD OF
BEAUTY ON ITS HANDS.[23]

And this was only what they had done to type.
Corrigan likewise described ornament as "an outbreak
of blains and wems, blotches and wens, pimple and
fungi, carbuncles and warts, and all manner of
excrescences."[24] The *Inland Printer* pronounced the
latest typographical "travesties" issued to letterpress
printers as appearing to be "laboring under a violent
attack of inflammatory rheumatism."[25] These verbal
pyrotechnics eventually cease to register as a critique
of taste or artistic sensibility; they seem to capture in
extremis a latent fear of contamination. Like
Shakespeare's Caliban or Dr. Frankenstein's monster,
decorated type and artistic ornament were hybrid,
unnatural, and deformed. *(Figures 91–99, 104)*

It was during the period of this typographical and
critical frenzy, the 1880s and 1890s, that critics also
began to speak of typography and design in gendered

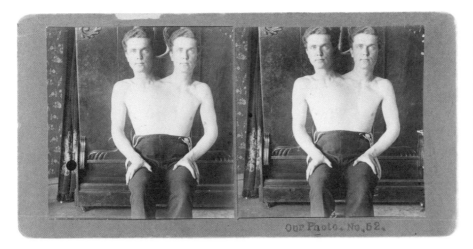

below: **Figure 102**
Portrait of Oscar Wilde by
Napoleon Sarony, ca. 1882

opposite: **Figure 103**
Banquet typeface, by Marder,
Luse & Co., ca. 1889
Extremely light, attenuated typefaces such as this were branded as feminine, or "weak and misty."

adjectives. Typography that whispered on the page in thin and "modern" or attenuated, ornamented faces that mocked utility were described as "feminine."[26] (*Figure 103*) Feminine typography was decorative, airy, tentative, and protean, and it catered to "new" readers, that is, women, immigrants, and the nouveau riche.

It was mass-produced and could be found in popular novels, as well as in the fancy gift books of inspiring poesy that graced nineteenth-century bourgeois parlors. In contrast, historicism, such as that of William Morris, was described as "masculine."[27] Masculinity supposedly lay in the darkness of his typefaces, in the tightness of his line spacing, and in his allegiance to historical letterforms. His page compositions sat like fortified blocks, surrounded by extravagant margins. His press, meanwhile, produced lavish, handwrought editions that were within the economic reach of only a select few. Morris's steadfast refusal to pander to popular taste, along with his rejection of industrial production, only added to the perceived virility of his persona.

This gendered characterization of typography was perfectly in keeping with the period's anxious reconsideration of masculinity. The feminized, aestheticized man—like feminine typography—gave way to a more vigorous, heroic one, of which larger-than-life figures such as Theodore Roosevelt became prime exemplars. (*Figures 102, 105, 107*) The link made between femininity and the thin, delicate typography that was widely favored and mass-produced echoes the relationship posited by others between femininity and the civilizing impulse.The fast rate of acculturation in the nineteenth

190

Banquet

PATENT APPLIED FOR.

Paragon (20 Point).

Meeting of the National Editorial Association

uable and Practical Papers were Read, the mor

25   will be presented   38

To our Readers in the near Future

Double Great Primer (36 Point).

merican Furnishing Emporiu

Art Decorations

Quaint English Ornaments

44 Point American Flags, $2.50 per Dozen

24 POINT   6 A 10 a $5 00

Doric Italic—For War Scare-Heads
Made also in 6, 8, 10, 12 and 18 Point Sizes

60 POINT   4 A 5 a $15 50

CUBA FREED

36 POINT   5 A 7 a $8 75

Spanish Flags Driven from Western Seas

48 POINT   4 A 5 a $10 75

BIG INDEMNITY

48 POINT   4 A 5 a $10 75

Patriots Happy!

36 POINT   5 A 7 a $8 75

PHILIPPINE ISLANDS

30 POINT   5 A 7 a $6 50

And Porto Rico Held under Stars and Stripes!

AMERICAN TYPE FOUNDERS COMPANY

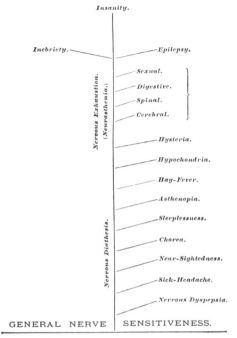

Insanity.

Inebriety. ——— | ——— Epilepsy.

Nervous Exhaustion. (Neurasthenia.)
— Sexual.
— Digestive.
— Spinal.
— Cerebral.

— Hysteria.

— Hypochondria.

— Hay-Fever.

— Asthenopia.

— Sleeplessness.

— Chorea.

— Near-Sightedness.

— Sick-Headache.

Nervous Diathesis.
— Nervous Dyspepsia.

GENERAL NERVE | SENSITIVENESS.

EVOLUTION OF NERVOUSNESS.

century, especially in America, was sometimes attributed to the civilizing effect of women, deemed the keepers of culture and manners and the "angels" of domestic serenity.

By the late nineteenth century, the feminine influence had started to appear symptomatic of cultural depletion. During the last third of the century a rising constellation of debilitating disorders began to present in women and upper-class men: that nebulous mental and physical diagnosis of "neurasthenia." In *American Nervousness*, Dr. George M. Beard's influential 1881 study of neurasthenia, dissipation (an undirected spending of "nerve force") eventually led to "decadence," a decay of the nerves in the individual and ultimately, it was thought, the decay of civilizations. (*Figure 106*) Dissipation was seen as a peculiarly American syndrome, made manifest as the country roared into the twentieth century—straining at the continental frontiers, overrun by waves of immigration, stretched by imperialist expansion, and bristling with industrial might. There was only so much "nerve force" in reserve, and one was not to squander it lightly. Cultural health was fragile, according to Beard:

> ALL OUR CIVILIZATION HANGS BY A THREAD; THE ACTIVITY AND FORCE OF THE VERY FEW MAKES US WHAT WE ARE AS A NATION; AND IF, THROUGH DEGENERACY, THE DESCENDENTS OF THESE FEW REVERT TO THE CONDITION OF THEIR NOT VERY REMOTE ANCESTORS, ALL OUR HAUGHTY CIVILIZATION WILL BE WIPED AWAY. [28]

Artistic printing, with its elaborately manipulated elements and surfeit of ornament, was categorically denounced as a waste of energy. As Loos later stated "Ornament is wasted labour power and hence wasted health…"[29] Artistic printing, it would seem, was to be excised from design history because it shared in ornament's "crime."

opposite: **Figure 105**
"Doric Italic—For War Scare-Heads" newspaper display type, from the American Type Founders Company, ca. 1898
The beau ideal of the sensitive aesthete was supplanted by self-conscious, nationalistic vigor in the changing cultural landscape of the late nineteenth century.

top: **Figure 106**
Diagram of nervous illness, from *American Nervousness*, by George M. Beard, M.D. (1881)
Neurasthenia was part of a growing atmosphere of diffuse anxiety about cultural and societal dilution.

above: **Figure 107**
Photomontage of Theodore Roosevelt, by Underwood & Underwood, 1908 (detail)

193

Conclusion

In the early 1990s, iconic modernist Massimo Vignelli
scoffed at the experimental graphic design magazine
Emigre, calling it an "aberration of culture" and a "typographic garbage factory." Most damning, Vignelli thought,
was that the magazine didn't take up the responsibility
of upholding society at large. *Emigre,* designer David
Carson, and other promulgators of typographical "inco-
herence" and design eccentricity were charged with
inciting a Cult of the Ugly, willfully steering design away
from the accepted canon and Paul Rand's mantra
of unity, harmony, grace and rhythm.

Two sets of typographic
ornaments designed in the
early 1990s and sold by *Emigre*
magazine exemplified a renewed
interest in ornament that
was novel and personal.
Ed Fella's enigmatic doodles,
reminiscent of nineteenth-
century combination ornaments,
became FellaParts in 1993
(left). Zuzana Licko's Whirligig
(above) updated traditional
printers' "flowers" in 1994.

The fractured, layered design and typographical experiments of the late 1980s
and '90s, spurred on by the freedom of the computer, weren't only lacking in
harmony, they were, in Vignelli's assessment, "just like freaking out." Emigre founder
Rudy VanderLans's reply was that his wish for graphic design was that it would expe-
rience "a return to design that is infused with local color and personal idiosyncrasies."[1]
By the time of the "Ugly" design debates, the turn away from ornament and expression
in serious design had been so ingrained that the idea of visual play, hybrid typefaces,
or tampering with legibility could indeed seem threatening. Again.

In her essay "The Crystal Goblet, or Printing Should be Invisible" from 1956,
typographer and scholar Beatrice Warde (1900–1969), a mainstay of graphic design
education, declared, "all good type is modernist."[2] Indeed, the essence of design-
school instruction for much of the twentieth century was reduction, refinement,
and the search for succinct, essential communication—strategies that left little room

195

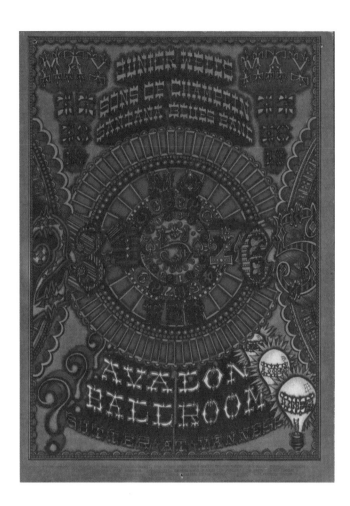

196

for expressiveness or the use of ornament. If good design was transparent, then artistic printing—and everything else now stamped "Victorian"—was thuddingly opaque.

The legacy of nineteenth-century artistic printing was that it spurred designers to run in the opposite direction. Beginning in the 1890s, design revivalists swept ornament off book pages, revived typefaces from the early years of printing, and analyzed the structure of page layout. In a grand turn away from eclecticism and expressiveness, type reformers and revivalists focused the anxieties about ornament that later came to be associated with modernism. The revival of fine printing did not become modernism, but shared with modernism a similar reaction to nineteenth-century popular taste and conducted a similar reappraisal of ornament. One movement looked backwards; the other forwards. Both left some room (albeit little) for the use of ornament; however, neither could find, as artistic printing had, that ornament was inherently necessary.

At the same time, a broad sifting of culture between high and low was taking place, with the removal of "high" culture to museums and conservatories. Job printing was cast in the "low" category, and it proceeded to lose ground from there on. Distinctions were drawn between professionally designed work and work produced by printers and amateurs. The latter joined the vast category of vernacular design. Commercial type design, an integral component of commercial job printing, fell in prestige. As Nicolete Gray described in her book *Nineteenth Century Ornamented Typefaces*, it

10 | DIGITAL HYBRID DIGITAL HYBRID DIGITAL HYBRID DIGITAL HYBRID DIGITAL HYBRID DIGITAL HYBRID

12 | DIGITAL HYBRID DIGITAL HYBRID DIGITAL HYBRID DIGITAL HYBRID DIGITAL HYBRID

16 | DIGITAL HYBRID DIGITAL HYBRID DIGITAL HYBRID DIGITAL HYE

24 | DIGITAL HYBRID DIGITAL HYBRID DIGITAL

36 | DIGITAL HYBRID DIGITAL HY

48 | DIGITAL HYBRID DIGI

60 | DIGITAL HYBRID

72 | DIGITAL HYBR

⟨HANDSOME NEW FACES.⟩

top: **Figure 109**
Time in Hell typeface, by Carlos Segura/T-26, 1994
Each letter of this digital hybrid font combines serif (Times) and sans serif (Helvetica) details.

middle: **Figure 110**
Stencil Gothic metal type, 1885
This nineteenth-century type mixes utilitarian and decorative elements.

below: **Figure 111**
Missionary typeface, designed by Miles Newlyn for *Emigre*, 1991
Line art found in Gothic decoration and OCR-A (a type designed in 1966 to be readable by computers), are both cited as inspirations for this digital hybrid font.

197

**Figure 112
Contemporary letterpress card,
by Hammerpress**
The recent revival of letterpress
printing relates to contemporary
interest in crafts and the DIY
movement. In modern letterpress
there is an almost fetishistic
emphasis on the handmade and
a quirky, subjective vision of
ornament.

was relegated "to popular magazine design, [and]
to chocolate-box and Christmas card decoration."[3]
In short, ephemera designed by printers was beneath
consideration. Design generally became a more solemn
affair, part religious service and part scientific discipline.

Playfulness and novelty did not disappear, though.
Throughout the twentieth century, rebellious designers
gravitated toward historical styles as a proclamation of
independence from mainstream functionalism. Music
posters in the 1960s mined vintage and hand-drawn
type with art nouveau–style illustrations. In the 1970s
there was a revival of interest in wood type, fancy types
of the nineteenth century, and commercial decorative
styles by young designers, such as the Pushpin Group,
fond of the vernacular past. In these instances, the
devalued remains of the nineteenth and early twentieth
centuries, free of their earlier cultural associations and
status, were available for easy appropriation.

Like the aesthetic movement of a century before,
postmodernism in the 1980s gave a late-in-the-century
intellectual justification for its "sampling" of history,
permitting the "high" end of design to explore and
reinterpret ornament. Postmodern or "pluralist" ornament tended to be geometric and nonrepresentational,
and found refuge from historicism in pattern making
and rational structure. Despite the new liberties of
postmodernism, literal historicism was never "meta"
enough, and ornament could be employed only with
explicit control and sufficient ironic distance.

Today, graphic design is as undogmatic as graphic design was in the 1870s or 1880s, but with modernist functionalism thrown into the mix. All styles are available for appropriation and inspiration. Much of the new ornament reveals the legacy of postmodernism and is heavily reliant on pattern, now easily constructed digitally. Where artistic printing was obsessed with borders and with edge definition, contemporary ornament is often made up of fields of pattern that bleed, overlap, and wrap surfaces. The recent resurgence of letterpress printing has swung attention to nineteenth-century investigations, and has increased appreciation of the brilliant effects of artistic printing. (*Figures 112—114*) Further curiosity about "Victorian" aesthetics has surfaced in the "steampunk" style of some contemporary fantasy fiction, which applies nineteenth-century aesthetics to an imaginary retro future. Steampunk and its allied DIY styles seem based in ambivalence about the present and support a reinvestigation of the value of handicrafts.

Sixteen years ago VanderLans had hoped for design to become infused with local color and personal idiosyncrasies, and in many ways, that has come to pass. Perhaps the current openness in graphic design can be sustained, or it may succumb, like artistic printing, to a stronger ideology. Given the number of professional graphic designers today, each exercising such freedom of expression, it is difficult to imagine them united by a common style. If this were to happen, it can be assumed to be a sign of much more dire changes in the culture.

Figure 113
Catalog for the California Institute of the Arts, 2007–09, by Jeffrey Keedy, 2007

Designer and educator Jeffrey Keedy's densely embellished catalog avoids what he termed "self-conscious" and "cool" hybrid asymmetry in favor of a "warm symmetrical, traditional style using ornament, decoration, and pattern that are exuberant, celebratory, inclusive, and pleasurable."

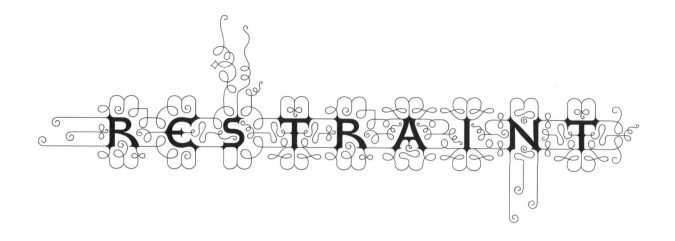

RESTRAINT

CAROLINE STITCHEM

RIDING HABITS · BALL DRESSES

UNDERWEAR · FURNISHING

top, bottom, and opposite:
Figure 114
Restraint typeface by
Marian Bantjes with Ross Mills,
for Tiro Typeworks, 2007

above: **Figure 115**
Arboret No. 2 type specimen,
1885

Illustrator and designer Marian
Bantjes's typeface is seamless
and organically decorative. Like
nineteenth century faces such as
Arboret No. 2, letters might be
thought of as the spaces between
ornament.

200

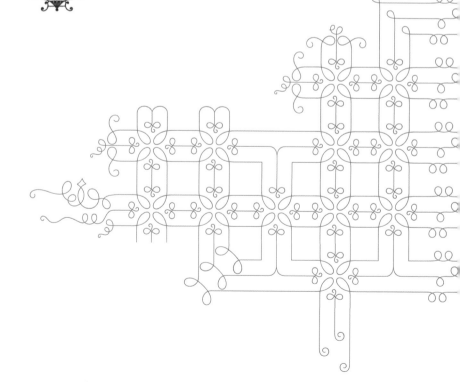

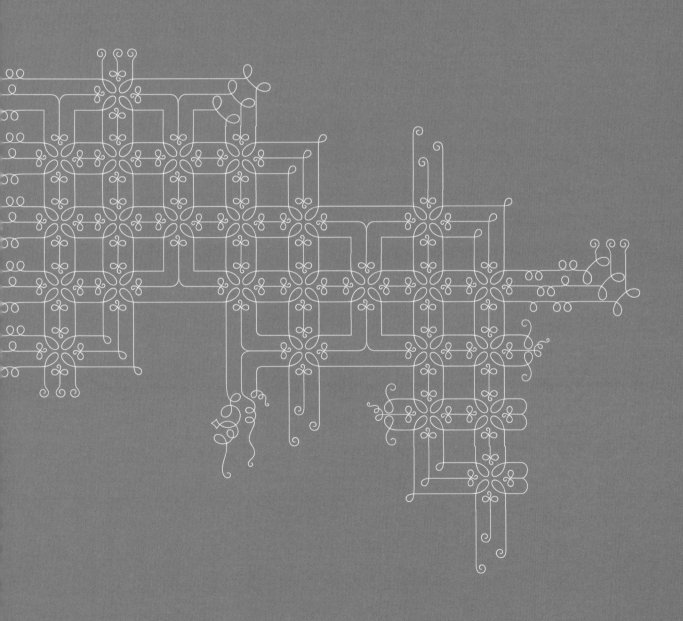

GREAT PRIMER .	And God said, L ▉
ENGLISH . . .	And God said, Let th ▉
PICA	And God said, Let there ▉
SMALL PICA .	And God said, Let there be ▉
LONG PRIMER .	And God said, Let there be li ▉
BOURGEOIS . .	And God said, Let there be light : ▉
BREVIER . .	And God said, Let there be light : a ▉
MINION . . .	And God said, Let there be light : and th ▉
NONPAREIL . .	And God said, Let there be light : and there ▉
PEARL . . .	And God said, Let there be light : and there was light. ▉

AMERICAN SYSTEM OF INTERCHANGEABLE TYPE BODIES.

No.	Name	No.	Name	No.	Name
1	American	14	English	40	Dbl. Paragon
1½	German				
2	Saxon	16	Columbian		
2½	Norse	18	Great Primer	44	Canon
3	Brilliant				
3½	Ruby	20	Paragon		
4	Excelsior			48	Four-Line Pica
4½	Diamond	22	Dbl. Small Pica		
5	Pearl				
5½	Agate	24	Double Pica		
6	Nonpareil			60	Five-Line Pica
7	Minion	28	Double English		
8	Brevier				
9	Bourgeois	32	Dbl. Columbian		
10	Long Primer			72	Six-Line Pica
11	Small Pica	36	Dbl. Grt. Primer		
12	Pica				

Historically, type was made to fit the bodies—the physical pieces of metal—used in each particular foundry that cast them. Sizes were designated with non-standardized names and typefaces made by different foundries would often vary so that they could not be used together efficiently.

The United States introduced the point system as a national standard in 1886, with type founders casting types in a uniform size and height from then on.

Notes

INTRODUCTION

1 The recent *New Typographic Design* (New Haven: Yale University Press, 2007) by Roger Fawcett-Tang introduces a survey of contemporary typography with a description of artistic printing that is more generous than usual.

2 Graham Hudson's *The Design and Printing of Ephemera in Britain and America, 1720–1920* (New Castle, DE and London: The British Library and Oak Knoll Press, 2008).

3 For British writers who have addressed artistic printing, see Nicolete Gray and Ray Nash (*Nineteenth Century Ornamented Typefaces* [Berkeley and Los Angeles: University of California Press, 1976]); Vivian Ridler ("Artistic Printing: A Search for Principles," in *Alphabet and Image* 6, [January 1948]); and David Jury (*Letterpress: New Applications for Traditional Skills* [Mies, CH: Rotovision, 2006]).

CHAPTER 1

1 Although this phrase originated in France in the early nineteenth century, Walter Pater's use of it in his 1873 book *The Renaissance: Studies in Art & Poetry* (London: MacMillan & Co.) placed it at the heart of the aesthetic movement in England.

2 Ellen Mazur Thomson, *The Origins of Graphic Design in America, 1870–1920* (New Haven: Yale University Press, 1997), 13.

3 *American Art Printer* IV, no. 11 (June 1891): 268.

4 Rob Roy Kelly, *American Wood Type, 1828–1900* (New York: Van Nostrand Reinhold Company, 1969), 191.

5 See Barbara Whitney Keyser, "Ornament as Idea: Indirect Imitation of Nature in the Design Reform Movement," *Journal of Design History* 11, no. 2 (1998).

6 Ibid., 136.

7 Michael Whiteway, *The Shock of the Old: Christopher Dresser's Design Revolution* (New York: Smithsonian, Cooper-Hewitt, National Design Museum, 2004), 48.

8 Another book by Michael Whiteway—*Christopher Dresser, 1834–1904* (Milan: Skira, 2001)—presents Dresser's work by manufacturer, which underscores its great range.

9 One of the first descriptions of Harpel's influence on style appears in the introduction to volume VI of *The Printers' International Specimen Exchange*, published in London by *The Paper and Printing Trades Journal* ([1885]: 3–4). Thereafter, *Harpel's Typograph, or Book of Specimens* (Cincinnati: self-published, 1870) has been accepted generally as a milestone in the beginning of artistic printing. The gensis of *Harpel's Typograph* in Cincinnati is not surprising, since centers of travel and commerce such as this gateway city to the American West provided many commissions for artistic printers. Newly established towns in Kansas, Texas, Colorado, and other western states often began newspapers with job printing offices that designed work in the latest style.

10 *Harpel's Typograph* was, for instance, sold in the catalogs of MacKellar, Smiths & Jordan. See the Philadelphia type foundry's "General Price Lists," 1877 to 1890, held in the American Type Founders Co. archive, Rare Book and Manuscript Library, Columbia University, New York. For the use of the book as a prize, see Walker Rumble, *The Swifts: Printers in the Age of Typesetting Races* (Charlottesville: University of Virginia Press, 2003), 166.

11 *The Printers' International Specimen Exchange* VI (1885): 3–4.

12 In this, *Harpel's Typograph* bears a resemblance to the 1841 book by noted British designer Owen Jones by the name of *Ancient Spanish Ballads* (rev. ed., translated with notes by J. G. Lockhart [London: J. Murray]). Regarded as one of the first publications of the nineteenth century to combine high standards of decoration, printing, and illustration, it may have served as a model for Harpel. Carol A. Hrvol Flores, *Owen Jones: Design, Ornament, Architecture, & Theory in an Age of Transition* (New York: Rizzoli, 2006), 38.

13 Rumble, 162.

14 The date of the beginning of Kelly's career in New York is unclear. The hagiographic biography that appeared in the *The American Art Printer* in 1891 leaves it so. The author of the biography, Howard Lyons, writes, "artistic printing began no earlier than the years 1860–65," however, his narrative chronicles Kelly's life—from his birth in Ireland to his moves to Canada and New York, culminating in his participation in the 1878 Exposition Universelle in Paris—without providing any dates. *The American Art Printer* IV, no. 11 (June 1891): 268–69.

15 Ibid., 268.

16 Ibid.

17 In 1879, for example, an issue of *The Paper and Printing Trades Journal* in London dedicated five pages to a review of fifty specimens, including three by Americans. This was reported in New York in the *American Model Printer* I, no. 2 (November 1879): 32.

18 Thomas Hailing to the Oxford Printing Works, Cheltenham, 15 September 1879, in *American Model Printer* I, no. 4 (January–February 1880): 51.

19 Henry Lewis Bullen, "Discursions of a Retired Printer—American Types Abroad and the Men Who Did Most to Establish Foreign Markets. Some Reflections and Suggestions Relating to the Foreign Trade in American Manufactures for Printing," *The Inland Printer* XXXVIII, no. 5 (February 1907): 675–77.

20 *American Model Printer* I, no. 8 (September–December 1880): 103.

21 *American Model Printer* I, no. 3 (December 1879): 40; and *American Model Printer* I, no. 9 (January–March 1881): 111.

22 *Oesterreichische Buchdrucker Zeitung* 45, quoted in *American Model Printer* I, no. 8 (September–December 1880): 103.

CHAPTER 2

1 Oscar H. Harpel, *Harpel's Typograph, or Book of Specimens* (Cincinnati: self-published, 1870), 17. Although Harpel desired to "inaugurate a better understanding of the tasteful utility as well as artistic scope of typography in the present day," he also promoted good craftsmanship because it aided "the advance to financial success" (3–4).

2 "English design schools were established in 1836 by English manufacturers to train skilled designers for industry. Only in the 1870s did Americans follow suit." Ellen Mazur Thomson, *The Origins of Graphic Design in America, 1870–1920* (New Haven: Yale University Press, 1997), 109.

3 For more on the selling of American typefaces overseas, see Henry Lewis Bullen, "Discursions of a Retired Printer," *The Inland Printer* XXXVIII, no. 5 (February 1907): 675–77.

4 The contemporary cost was figured with the inflation calculator at www.westegg.com/inflation/. The calculator's pre-1975 data are the Consumer Price Index statistics from *Historical Statistics of the United States* (Washington, DC: U.S. Government Printing Office, 1975). All data since then are from the annual *Statistical Abstracts of the United States* (Washington, DC: U. S. Census Bureau).

5 *American Model Printer*, *The American Art Printer*, and *The Superior Printer* all advertised and discussed wrinklers and twisters.

CHAPTER 3

1 *The Printers' International Specimen Exchange* VIII (1887): 4–5.

2 "The Fitness of Things," *The American Art Printer* 2, no. 4 (July–August 1888): 3.

3 The last volume of *The Printers' International Specimen Exchange* appeared in 1896; of *The American Art Printer*, in 1893; of *The Superior Printer*, ca. 1890; and of *Art Age*, in 1889. *The Inland Printer* adapted to the changing stylistic ethos by focusing on technology and continued into the twentieth century. It is still published today as *American Printer* magazine.

4 Clarence P. Hornung, ed., *Will Bradley: His Graphic Art* (New York: Dover, 1974), xix–xx.

5 Henry Lewis Bullen, "William Morris, Regenerator of the Typographic Art," *The Inland Printer* LXIX (June 1922): 372.

6 Clarence P. Hornung, *Handbook of Early American Advertising Art* (New York: Dover, 1947), xxxix.

7 Frank Denman, *The Shaping of Our Alphabet* (New York: Alfred A. Knopf, 1955), 179.

8 Andrew J. Corrigan, *A Printer and His World* (London: Faber & Faber, 1944), 124.

9 Ibid., 98.

10 Ibid., 113, 120–21.

11 Wilbur Fisk Cleaver, *Five Centuries of Printing: A Compilation of Important Events in the History of Typography*, second edition (Johnstown, PA: self-published, 1932), 25.

12 Ibid.

13 For more on Morris's relationship to aestheticism, see Linda Dowling, *The Vulgarization of Art: The Victorians and Aesthetic Democracy* (Charlottesville: University of Virginia Press, 1996), especially chpt. 4.

14 Daniel Berkeley Updike, *Printing Types: Their History, Forms, and Use*, vol. 2 (New York: Dover, 1980), 205.

15 Fiona MacCarthy, *William Morris: A Life for Our Time* (New York: Alfred A. Knopf, 1995), 121.

16 Stanley Morison, "On the Classification of Typographical Variations," in *Letter Forms, Typographic and Scriptorial* (Vancouver, BC: Hartley & Marks, 1997), 66.

17 Ibid.

18 For interesting examples of Caslon and the Chiswick Press, see Updike, vol. 2, chpt. 21; A. F. Johnson, "Old-Face Types in the Victorian Age," *The Monotype Recorder* 30, no. 242 (September–December 1931): 5; and John Southward, *Progress in Printing and the Graphic Arts During the Victorian Era* (London: Simpkin, Marshall, Hamilton, Kent & Co., 1897), 19, 62–63.

CHAPTER 4

1 See, respectively, Andrew J. Corrigan, *A Printer and His World* (London: Faber & Faber, 1944), 6; *American Model Printer* I, no. 10 (April–June 1881): 130; and *The American Art Printer* 2, no. 2 (March–April 1888): 1.

2 R. H. Patterson, "Battle of the Styles," in his *Essays in History and Art* (London: William Blackwood and Sons, 1862), 331–39.

3 Corrigan, 102.

4 Ibid., 25.

5 James Trilling, *Ornament: A Modern Perspective* (Seattle: University of Washington Press, 2003), 138–41.

6 "Book Titles," in *Art Age* I, no. 3 (October 1883): 17.

7 This phrase appeared in almost all nineteenth-century printing texts, from type catalogs to printing manuals. It was based on an inscription on the facade of the house of fifteenth-century printer Laurent Koster in Haarlem, the Netherlands. Koster may have invented movable type before Gutenberg. The original Latin inscription read, in translation, "Sacred to the memory of Typography, the art conservator of all arts. Here first invented about the year 1440." William S. Walsh, *Handy-Book of Literary Curiosities* (Philadelphia: J. B. Lippincott, 1893), 68–69.

8 Marvin Fisher, *Workshops in the Wilderness: The European Response to American Industrialization, 1830–1860* (New York: Oxford University Press, 1967), 181.

9 Ibid., 180–81.

10 Gottfried Semper, "Science, Industry and Art: Proposals for the Development of a National Taste in Art at the Closing of the London Industrial Exhibition" (1852), reprinted in *The Four Elements of Architecture and Other Writings*, trans. H. F. Mallgrave and W. Herrmann (Cambridge: Cambridge University Press, 1989), 135.

11 Linda Dowling, *The Vulgarization of Art: The Victorians and Aesthetic Democracy* (Charlottesville: University of Virginia Press, 1996), 90. Dowling speaks specifically about England, but her assessments hold true for America as well.

12 "Notes on Practice," *Art Age* I, no. 12 (July 1884): 136.

13 Egon Friedell, *A Cultural History of the Modern Age*, vol. 2 (New York: Alfred A. Knopf, 1930–32), 299–300, quoted in Allan Janik and Stephen Toulmin, *Wittgenstein's Vienna* (New York: Simon and Schuster, 1973), 97.

14 Janik and Toulmin, 98.

15 Adolph Loos, "Ornament and Crime" (1908), in *The Theory of Decorative Art: An Anthology of European & American Writings, 1750–1940*, ed. Isabelle Frank (New Haven: Yale University Press, 2000), 291.

16 Nikolaus Pevsner, *Pioneers of Modern Design: From William Morris to Walter Gropius* (1936, originally published under the title *Pioneers of the Modern Movement, from William Morris to Walter Gropius;* rev. ed. London: Penguin Books, 1960), 20–21.

17 Michael Whiteway, ed., *The Shock of the Old: Christopher Dresser's Design Revolution* (New York: Smithsonian, Cooper-Hewitt, National Design Museum, 2004), 21.

18 An article from the *Scottish Typographical Circular*, reprinted in *The American Art Printer* 3, no. 1 (May–June, 1889): 4.

19 Herbert Spencer, *Pioneers of Modern Typography* (1969; rev. ed. Cambridge, MA: MIT Press, 1983), 15.

20 Loos, quoted in Frank, ed., 290–91.

21 Trilling, "Transformation is the Essence of Ornament," in his *Ornament*, 153.

22 "Two Extremes," in the April 1885 issue of *The Inland Printer*, reproduced in *A Typographic Journey Through the Inland Printer, 1883–1900,* compiled by Maurice Annenberg (Baltimore: Maran Press, 1977), 48.

23 Corrigan, 100–2.

24 Ibid., 102

25 "Two Extremes," reproduced in *A Typographic Journey,* 48.

26 George M. Beard, *American Nervousness* (New York: G. P. Putnam's Sons, 1881), vi–ix.

27 Loos, quoted in Frank, ed., 291.

CONCLUSION

1 Egon Karol, interview with Rudy VanderLans, editor of *Emigre* magazine. Edited by Diane Burns. At www.ginkopress.com.

2 Beatrice Warde, "Printing Should Be Invisible," lecture first presented in 1930 and published in the same year in *The British and Colonial Printer & Stationer*. Reprinted under the title "The Crystal Goblet, or Printing Should Be Invisible," in *The Crystal Goblet: Sixteen Essays on Typography,* ed. Henry Jacob (London: Sylvan Press, 1955).

3 Nicolete Gray and Ray Nash, *Nineteenth Century Ornamented Typefaces* (Berkeley: University of California Press, 1976), 108–9.

Bibliography

American Art Printer, The (New York: C. E. Bartholomew), 1887–1893.

American Model Printer (New York: Kelly & Bartholomew), 1879–1885.

American Printers' Specimen Exchange, The (Buffalo: Ed. McClure), four volumes between 1886 and 1890.

Annenberg, Maurice. *A Typographic Journey Through The Inland Printer, 1883–1900*. Baltimore: Maran Press, 1977.

———. *Type Foundries of America and Their Catalogs*. New Castle, DE: Oak Knoll Press, 1994.

Beard, George M. *American Nervousness*. New York: G. P. Putnam's Sons, 1881

Benton, Megan L. "Typography and Gender: Remasculating the Modern Book." In *Illuminating Letters: Typography and Literary Interpretation*. Ed. Paul Gutjahr and Megan I. Benton. Amherst: University of Massachusetts Press, 2001.

Bøe, Alf. *From Gothic Revival to Functional Form: A Study in Victorian Theories of Design*. Oslo: Oslo University Press, 1957.

Cleaver, Wilbur Fisk. *Five Centuries of Printing: A Compilation of Important Events in the History of Typography*, second edition. Johnston, PA: self-published, 1932.

Corrigan, Andrew J. *A Printer and His World*. London: Faber and Faber, 1944.

Denman, Frank. *The Shaping of Our Alphabet*. New York: Alfred A. Knopf, 1955.

De Vinne, Theodore Low. "Masculine Printing." In *The American Bookmaker* 15 (November 1892): 140–44.

———. *Printing in the Nineteenth Century*. New York: Lead Mould Electrotype Foundry, 1924 (originally published in the *New York Evening Post*, 12 January 1901).

Dowling, Linda. *The Vulgarization of Art: The Victorians and Aesthetic Democracy*. Charlottesville: University of Virginia Press. 1996.

Dresser, Christopher. *Principles of Victorian Decorative Design*. New York: Dover, 1995 (originally published as *Principles of Decorative Design* in 1873).

———. *Studies in Design*. Layton, UT: Gibbs Smith, 2002 (first published in 1874).

Earhart, John F. *The Color Printer, A Treatise on the Use of Colors in Typographic Printing*. Cincinnati: Earhart and Richardson, 1892.

Fisher, Marvin. *Workshops in the Wilderness: The European Response to American Industrialization, 1830–1860*. New York: Oxford University Press, 1967.

Friedell, Egon. *A Cultural History of the Modern Age*. Three vols. New York: Alfred A. Knopf, 1930–32.

Gere, Charlotte, and Michael Whiteway. *Nineteenth-Century Design, from Pugin to Mackintosh*. New York: Harry N. Abrams, 1993.

Gray, Nicolete, and Ray Nash. *Nineteenth Century Ornamented Typefaces*. Berkeley: University of California Press, 1976.

Harpel, Oscar H. *Harpel's Typograph, or Book of Specimens Containing Useful Information, Suggestions, and a Collection of Examples of Letterpress Job Printing Arranged for the Assistance of Master Printers, Amateurs, Apprentices, and Others*. Cincinnati: self-published, 1870.

Hornung, Clarence. *Handbook of Early American Advertising Art*. New York: Dover, 1947.

———, ed. *Will Bradley: His Graphic Art*. New York: Dover, 1974.

Hudson, Graham. "Artistic Printing: A Reevaluation." *Journal*, n.s., 9 (2006): 31–63.

Inland Printer, The (Chicago: MacLean-Hunter), 1883–1958.

Janik, Allan, and Stephen Toulmin. *Wittgenstein's Vienna*. New York: Simon and Schuster, 1973.

Johnston, Alastair. *Alphabets to Order: The Literature of Nineteenth-Century Typefounders' Specimens*. New Castle, DE: Oak Knoll Press and the British Library, 2000.

Jones, Owen. *The Grammar of Ornament*. London: Day and Son, 1856.

Jury, David. *Letterpress: New Applications for Traditional Skills*. Mies, CH: Rotovision, 2006.

Kelly, Rob Roy. *American Wood Type, 1828–1900*. New York: Van Nostrand Reinhold, 1969.

Keyser, Barbara Whitney. "Ornament as Idea: Indirect Imitation of Nature in the Design Reform Movement." *Journal of Design History* 11, no. 2 (1998): 127–44.

Kinross, Robin. *Modern Typography: An Essay in Critical History*. London: Hyphen Press, 1992.

Lambourne, Lionel. *Japonisme: Cultural Crossings Between Japan and the West*. New York: Phaidon Press, 2005.

Levine, Lawrence W. *Highbrow Lowbrow: The Emergence of Cultural Hierarchy in America*. Cambridge, MA: Harvard University Press, 1988.

Lichten, Frances. *Decorative Art of Victoria's Era*. New York: Charles Scribner's Sons, 1950.

Lutz, Tom. *American Nervousness, 1903: An Anecdotal History*. Ithaca, NY: Cornell University Press, 1991.

Lynes, Russel. *The Tastemakers: The Shaping of American Popular Taste*. New York: Dover, 1980 (originally published by Harper & Brothers in 1955).

206

MacCarthy, Fiona. *William Morris: A Life for Our Time*. New York: Alfred A. Knopf, 1995.

MacKellar, Thomas. *The American Printer: A Manual of Typography*. Fourth edition. Philadelphia: MacKellar, Smiths & Jordan, 1868.

Montana, Andrew. *The Art Movement in Australia: Design, Taste and Society, 1875–1900*. Victoria, Australia: The Miegunyah Press, 2000.

Morison, Stanley. *Letter Forms, Typographic and Scriptorial: Two Essays on Their Classification, History, and Bibliography*. Vancouver, BC: Hartley & Marks, 1997 (essays first published between 1963 and 1968).

Printers' International Specimen Exchange, The (London: Office of *The Paper and Printing Trades Journal*, 1880–1887; and Office of *The British Printer*, 1888–1898).

Rant. Special issue, *Emigre* 64. New York: Princeton Architectural Press, 2003.

Ridler, Vivian. "Artistic Printing: A Search for Principles." *Alphabet and Image* 6 (January 1948): 4–17.

Robinson, Elrie. *Horse and Buggy Printing*. St. Francisville, LA: self-published, 1939.

Rumble, Walker. *The Swifts: Printers in the Age of Typesetting Races*. Charlottesville: University of Virginia Press, 2003.

Semper, Gottfried, "Science, Industry, and Art: Proposals for the Development of a National Taste in Art at the Closing of the London Industrial Exhibition" (1852), reprinted in *The Four Elements of Architecture and Other Writings*, trans. H. F. Mallgrave and W. Herrmann. Cambridge: University Press, 1989, 130–67.

Southward, John. *Artistic Printing*. London: Printer's Register Office, 1892.

———. *Modern Printing: A Treatise on the Principles and Practice of Typography and the Auxiliary Arts*. London: Raithby, Lawrence & Co., 1899.

Specimens of Printing Types, Border, Cuts, Rules, &c. Philadelphia: MacKellar, Smiths & Jordan, 1868.

Spencer, Herbert. *Pioneers of Modern Typography*. Cambridge: MIT Press, 2004.

Superior Printer, The (Cincinnati: Earhart and Richardson), 1887–ca. 1890.

Thompson, Susan Otis. *American Book Design and William Morris*. New York: R. R. Bowker, 1977.

Thomson, Ellen Mazur. *The Origins of Graphic Design in America, 1870–1920*. New Haven: Yale University Press, 1997.

Trilling, James. *Ornament: A Modern Perspective*. Seattle: University of Washington Press, 2003.

Updike, Daniel Berkeley. *Printing Types: Their History, Forms, and Use. A Study in Survivals*. New York: Dover, 1980 (unabridged replication of the 1937 second edition, as published by Harvard University Press, Cambridge).

Wallis, Lawrence. "George W. Jones, Printer Laureate," Friends of the St. Bride Printing Library, second annual conference, London, October 2003.

Whiteway, Michael, ed. *The Shock of the Old: Christopher Dresser's Design Revolution*. New York: Smithsonian, Cooper-Hewitt, National Design Museum, 2004.

Whybrew, Samuel. *The Progressive Printer: A Book of Instruction for Journeymen and Apprenticed Printers*. Rochester, NY: Whybrew & Ripley, 1882.

Wood, Robert. *Victorian Delights*. London: Evans Brothers, 1967.

Typefaces

Rather than displaying a full alphabet of upper and lower case letters, nineteenth-century type specimens were composed in the form of mock advertisements or humorous epigrams. Livelier versions of today's "quick brown fox...," these samples were usually fanciful, often witty, and, on occasion, offensive.

Seated around large polishing stones, workers in the Rubbing and Dressing Department of the Mackellar, Smiths & Jordan type foundry smooth burrs from newly cast individual pieces of type, ca. 1890.

THE MFG. CO. — Patent Pending.

8A, 16a.   THREE-LINE NONPAREIL ALPINE. $3.65

❈ CRICKET & SPECKLED SPIDER
What's this Bug Traveling up My Coat-sleeve
$ 1234567890 ?

6A, 12a.   DOUBLE PICA ALPINE. $4.35

❈ CURVING LOVELINESS
Quaint Conceits of Modern Designs
❈ 1234567890 ❈

4A, 8a.   THREE-LINE PICA ALPINE. $5.80

BRONTE & CO.
Makers of Fictitous Men
❈ 1234567890 ❈

HAVE ADDED THREE-LINE NONPAREIL SIZE NOT SHOWN IN FORMER ISSUES

Six-line Nonpareil.   36-POINT VICTORIA.   6A, $6.75

FREAKS · OF · NATURE
✳ MENAGERIES ✳

Four-line Nonpareil.   24-POINT VICTORIA.   8A, $4.50

HIGHER ✳ MOUNTS ✳ CLIMBED
✳ PROCURE · EXERCISE ✳

Three-line Nonpareil.   18-POINT VICTORIA.   10A, $3.50

EXPLAIN · METEOROLOGICAL · REPORTS
SCIENTISTS ✳ 365 ✳ OBSERVING

New English.   14-POINT VICTORIA.   12A, $3.25

MARBLE ✳ TOMBSTONE
✳ CENOTAPH ✳
BURIAL · CUSTOMS

Two-line Nonpareil.   12-POINT VICTORIA.   16A, $3.00

INCINERATION ✳ ADVANCING
✳ PROGRESSIVE ✳
ERECT · CREMATORIES

New Long Primer.   10-POINT VICTORIA.   20A, $2.75

CONCERT ✳ PROGRAMME ✳ PRINTING
✳ PECULIAR FASHIONS ✳
SUPERIOR · WORKMANSHIP · 24

New Brevier.   8-POINT VICTORIA.   28A, $2.50

FORLORN ✳ HABITATION ✳ AND ✳ SIMPLE ✳ HABITS
✳ HUMBLE HERMIT DISTURBED ✳
ENDURANCE · OF · STRICT · SOLITUDE · 180

— VICTORIA —

The Victoria Series, being cut systematically, lines in the several ways here shown. Neither cardboard nor paper required in combining the different sizes with each other; use Point Standard Leads and Slugs in justifying.

HHHHHHHHHHHHH ✳ NEAT ✳ FACE ✳ HHHHHHHHHHHH

CAST BY THE CENTRAL TYPE FOUNDRY, ST. LOUIS, MO.

THE BARB SERIES.

Sorrow stings like the Thrust of an Envenomed Barb.

The Decoration Day Parade.

$1234567890.

BARB STEEDS

Running with Speed and Endurance.

GREAT SUMMER TRAVEL.

$1234567890.

Our Prices will meet competitive rates for Cash—all sales on satisfactory terms—while the well-known excellence of Our Manufacture will be scrupulously maintained.

FARMER, LITTLE & CO., NEW YORK AND CHICAGO.

CRITERION.

COVERED BY PATENT OF ◊ AUGUST 12, 1884.

12A, 24a,	Pica (12 Points Standard Measure).	$2.85

LADIES' SEWING CIRCLE
Meets · Tuesdays · and · Fridays · for
Business and Pleasure
24 Scandalous Gossip 58

8A, 16a,	Great Primer (18 Points Standard Measure).	$3.75

MUSICAL · VOICES
Those Strains Melodious
3 Night Owls 6

»» SHARP AND FINDEM, ««
Fire, · Life, · and · Marine
Insurance · Agents
25 High Premium St. 25
◦◦◦
All Claims for Losses Vigorously Contested.

6A, 12a,	Double Pica (24 Points Standard Measure).	$4.50

»» HOWLING · TAX-EATERS ««
42 Schemes · for · Depleting · Treasuries 38

4A, 8a,	Double Great Primer (36 Points Standard Measure).	$6.50

LAND AND WATER
The Art of making Mud Pies

ORNAMENTS AND FIGURES WITH ALL SIZES.   SPACES AND QUADS WITH ALL SIZES EXCEPT PICA.

Marder, Luse & Co., Type Founders, Chicago.

EBONY.

PATENT APPLIED FOR.

8A, 16a,   Great Primer (18 Point). $4.75

NIGHT, SABLE GODDESS

From her Ebony Throne, in Rayless Majesty Stretches
234 Forth her Leaden Scepter 567

6A, 12a,   Double Pica (24 Point). $4.75

MANNING & WOOD

Railroad and Commercial Printers
26 Broadway 28

4A, 8a   Double Great Primer (36 Point). $7.25

WORLD'S FAIR

Chicago the Peoples Choice 93

3A, 6a,   Four-Line Pica (48 Point). $9.75

Anniversary
Discovery of America

FIGURES AND LOGOTYPES WITH ALL SIZES.   SPACES AND QUADS EXTRA.

10A.   THREE-LINE NONPAREIL IDEAL $2.85
Quads and Spaces. 38c.

CUYAHOGA'S
SHADY SUMMER GROVE
EXCURSIONS

7A   DOUBLE PICA IDEAL. $3.00

SYLVAN
TROUT STREAMS
PISCATORIAL

5A.   THREE-LINE PICA IDEAL. $4.80

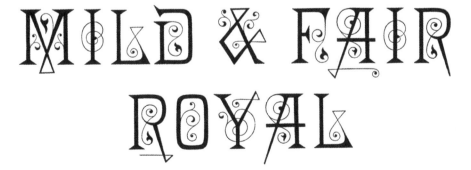

MILD & FAIR
ROYAL

Indestructible Type Company

491-493 CARROLL AVE., CHICAGO.

48-point Indestructible Script.   (24-point in preparation.)   4 A, 10 a. $12.00.

Indestructible Script combines Beauty and Usefulness.

PATENT PENDING.

PATENT PENDING FOR THE LINDSAY TYPE FOUNDRY.

7 A. 14 a.   THREE LINE NONPAREIL (18 POINT) MATHILDE.   Price $3.75.

KALAMAZOO & OSHKOSH

Startling Vagaries of a Brilliant Imagination

WISCONSIN & 1835

6 A. 12 a.   DOUBLE PICA (24 POINT) MATHILDE.   Price $5.00.

DAKOTA & BLIZZARDS

Flowers & From & The & Mountains

SUNDAY 1764

PICA AND THREE-LINE PICA SIZES WILL BE READY WHEN THIS APPEARS

955. DOUBLE GREAT PRIMER KISMET, 6 a, 3 A, $4.50.

THE PURITAN & GENESTA

Grand Ocean Races

Showing Excellent Speed

NEW ORNAMENTS.

1. Double   Paragon.   2. Double Paragon.   2.   1. Double   Paragon.

10 Cents Each.   10 Cents Each.

3. Long Primer, 15 cents per set.   4. Great Primer, 25 cents per set.   5. Pica, 20 cents per set.

DOWN BY AULD KIRK HOME

Left on the 31st on Foot

Miss Jumbo's Friday Primp

ANGLICAN
LIGHT ᛫ MEDIAEVAL.
No. TWO.

Patented   Aug. 9, '81

| 10 A 15 A 20 a, | PICA ANGLICAN No. 2 | $4.85 | | 8 A 12 A 20 a, | GREAT PRIMER ANGLICAN No. 2 | $6.75 |

⇥SPANISH᛫CASTLE⇤
The Corsican Brothers of Elbe
93 ⇥CARLISTS⇤ 42

⇥FAIRY ᛫ TALES.⇤
Mother ᛫ Goose's ᛫ Fables.
24 CHILDREN. 13

6 A 8 A 12 a,   DOUBLE PICA ANGLICAN No. 2 $8.50.

⇥JASON'S᛫GOLDEN᛫ARGOSY⇤
Sketches ᛫ from ᛫ Late ᛫ Venecian ᛫ History
4   THE HERMITAGE   3

CAST FROM LIGHT MEDIAEVAL. ORIGINAL MATRICES.
PATENTED AUG. 9, 1881.

| 10 A 20 a, | PICA LIGHT MEDIÆVAL. | $3.65 | | 10 A 20 a, | GREAT PRIMER LIGHT MEDIÆVAL. | $5.50 |

⇥GEORGIA FARMS⇤
Diary of our Wild Adventures
37 Far West 86

⇥BROADWAY⇤
Grand Republican Army
27 Politics 48

8 A 12 a,   DOUBLE PICA LIGHT MEDIÆVAL. $6.05

⇥AN AMERICAN SOLDIER⇤
History and Anecdotes of the Late War
7 Musical Festival 5

PICA ANGLICAN No. 2 AND LIGHT MEDIÆVAL, IN COMBINATION.
CHARGE OF THE LIGHT BRIGADE--NOBLE SIX HUNDRED

GREAT PRIMER ANGLICAN No. 2 AND LIGHT MEDIÆVAL, IN COMBINATION.
GREAT HOGGARTY DIAMOND FIELD

DOUBLE PICA ANGLICAN No. 2 AND LIGHT MEDIÆVAL, IN COMBINATION.
WONDROUS ᛫ ALCON ᛫ MYTHOLOGY.

JAMES CONNER'S SONS NEW YORK.

MODOC.

PATENTED AUG. 12, 1884.

12A, 24a,   PICA. (12 Points Standard Measure. $2.50

EXTENSIVE COLLECTION OF WORKS OF ART FOR SALE

Comprising Many Choice Productions of both the Old Masters and Old Maids

Including the Famous "Horse Fair," by Joe Key

24 TO BE DISPOSED OF WITHOUT RESERVE 76

8A, 16a,   GREAT PRIMER. (18 Points Standard Measure.) $3.40

THE FINE ART STATIONERY Co

Engravers and Printers, Chromo-Lithographers, etc.

Unique Designs in Cards and Envelopes

6A, 12a,   DOUBLE PICA. (24 Points Standard Measure.) $4.60

YE PENSIVE MAIDEN

A Playntive Ballade of ye 16th Centurie

By Poet Softheart Weepington

4A, 8a,   DOUBLE GREAT PRIMER. (36 Points Standard Measure.) $6.30

DANGER AHEAD

Most Thrilling Narrative 8

FIGURES AND ORNAMENTS WITH ALL SIZES.   SPACES AND QUADS WITH ALL SIZES EXCEPT PICA.

STIPPLE

REGISTERED, No. 141,760.

PATENTED FEB. 18, 1890.

THREE-LINE PICA.   36 POINT STIPPLE.   7 A, $5.35.

GRAPHIC DELINEATION

THE RAGGED EDGES OF POVERTY

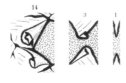

1234567890

FOUR-LINE PICA.   48 POINT STIPPLE.   6 A, $6.90.

METEMPSYCHOSIS

DISCARDED WRITINGS

12345678

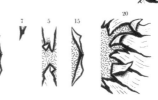

STIPPLE SERIES SHOWN IN COMBINATION.

TAGRAG SCOLLOP COMPANY

The MacKellar, Smiths & Jordan Co., Philadelphia.   Shniedewend & Lee Co., Agents, Chicago, Ill.

Novelty  *Script.*

ORIGINAL.

4a 3A — 72-POINT NOVELTY SCRIPT. — $16.00

Beatrice Granger

Nature's Child

5a 3A — 60-POINT NOVELTY SCRIPT. — $11.75

Whistling Heathens

Love is Blind

6a 3A — 48-POINT NOVELTY SCRIPT. — $9.00

King's Lake

Cat Fish

8a 4A — 36-POINT NOVELTY SCRIPT. — $7.25

Happy Dreams

Night Time

12a 5A — 24-POINT NOVELTY SCRIPT. — $5.25

Beauties of the Vintage

Pure Grape Juice

16a 5A — 18-POINT NOVELTY SCRIPT. — $4.00

Vice Stings Even in Our Pleasure

Field of Golden Clover

CAST BY CENTRAL TYPE FOUNDRY, ST. LOUIS.
For Sale by all Foundries and Branches of the American Type Founders' Co.

$2.60. 12-POINT ORNAMENTED, No. 1,566. 30 a and 15 A
2 lb. 4 oz.

Manual of the Corporation of the City of New York, with Maps, Plans and Specifications

The American Magazine and Repository of Useful Literature, devoted to Science, Literature and Art, Embellished with many Engravings

PERSONAL RECOLLECTIONS OF THE STAGE.   NOTICES OF ACTORS.   AMOUNT DUE $2,679

$4.00. 18-POINT ORNAMENTED, No. 1,566. 25 a and 12 A
4 lb.

Exploration of the Valley of the Amazon River made under the Direction of the Navy Department

AMERICAN LIFE INSURANCE COMPANY OF PHILADELPHIA, $75,000.

$5.15. 24-POINT ORNAMENTED, No. 1,566. 20 a and 10 A
5 lb. 12 oz.

Medicines in themselves are really Mischievous and Destructive of Nature.

AMERICAN SAVINGS INSTITUTE.   BALANCE 1894

$6.35. 36-POINT ORNAMENTED, No. 1,566. 15 a and 8 A
7 lb. 12 oz.

Special Departments to Represent each Branch of our Business

ARTICLES SUITABLE TO THE TRADE, 1894

$8.80. 48-POINT ORNAMENTED, No. 1,566. 12 a and 7 A
12 lb. 4 oz.

Printing Types at Reduced Prices. Estimates given

TYPE-FOUNDRY, 13 CHAMBERS-ST.

Baltimore Type Foundry.

Charles J. Cary & Co., No. 116 Bank Lane, Baltimore, Md.

PATENTED.

10-POINT RHOMBIC. 15 A 40 a $2 15
HANDSOME RIVERSIDE COTTAGE
Meagre Talkers 123 Ungraceful Heads

12-POINT RHOMBIC. 15 A 15 A 25 a $3 10
EXCELLENT TICKETHOLDER
Remember his 234 Money Return

18-POINT RHOMBIC. 12 A 12 A 18 a $4 30
VALUABLE HINTS TO YOUNG MEN AND WOMEN
Recommend Honesty on 235 The Grounds of its Being

24-POINT RHOMBIC. 10 A 10 A 15 a $6 00
THE GOVERNMENT PRINTING OFFICE
Respect Yourself 257 Fair Wages Paid

36-POINT RHOMBIC. 4 A 5 A 8 a $6 00
ANARCHIST IMPORTANCE
The Process 124 Descriptions

18-POINT EASTER. PATENTED. 8 A 20 a $3 00
Extra Lower case, $1 50
Opening Day. Autumn. September, 29, 1886.

The Only Practical Stereotype Outfits.

Special Attention Given. Winter. Descriptive Circular.

24-POINT EASTER. 6 A 14 a $3 75
Extra Lower case, $1 75
Sole Agents. Smith, Jones & Brothers.

Manufacturers, Jobbers and Dealers.

NOTE.—In view of the action of the Type Founders' Convention, held October 26th, recognizing the point system, we wish to call attention to the fact, that we were the first Foundry with an established plant to announce to the printers of the United States, that the point system would be THE SYSTEM of the future, and we went to a very heavy expense in making new moulds and altering matrices to adopt it in our Foundry.

LONDON * PARIS * BERLIN * VIENNA

Pleasant and Invigorating Wanderings on Summer Mornings through Central Park

Metropolitan Museum : Obelisk : Grotto : Terrace : Belvidere : Ramble

SEPTEMBER 1874-76

THE YEOMAN OF THE GUARD

Gilbert and Sullivan's New Comic Opera

Produced : at : the : Savoy : Theatre, : London : October : 3rd.

A * GREAT * HIT * 1884

SENATE CHAMBER

Evening : Sessions : held : at : Washington : D.C.

SUMMER * 1867

WEST POINT ACADEMY

Flirtation : Walk : by : Moonlight

CLASS * OF * '84

ZINCO.

REGISTERED, No. 165,803.

PATENTED MAR. 3, 1891.

12 POINT ZINCO.   10 A, 28 a, $3.50

· CURIOSITIES ·   Persons Accepting Misfortune with Smiling Countenances
·· OUTSIDE ··   Cheerfully Arising when Knocked Down by Adversity
·· OF THE ··   Blithesome, Vivacious, Laughter-provoking Associates
· DIME · MUSEUM ·   Ever Finding Brightness in Character and Surroundings

24 POINT ZINCO.   5 A, 14 a, $4.30

Unobtrusive · Specimens · of · Benevolence

Opulence and Penury Walking Arm-in-Arm

Missionaries Labouring Among Politicians

· 1234567890 ·

18 POINT ZINCO.   8 A, 20 a, $3.95

· PAUL · PRY ·   Thoroughly Acquainted with Family History
·· THE ··   Retailer of Gossip Probable and Improbable
· VILLAGE ·   Counsellor in Matters Trivial or Momentous
SIR · ORACLE   Author and Publisher of Fictitious Incidents

36 POINT ZINCO.   4 A, 10 a, $6.25

Kettle=Drumming and Locomotive Whistling

Calithumpia · Banging · Association

ALL COMPLETE WITH FIGURES.

The MacKellar, Smiths & Jordan Co. { Nos. 606-614 Sansom Street, Philadelphia.
Western Branch: 328-330 Dearborn Street, Chicago.

Mikado Series.

-THE- MFG Patent Pending.

6A, 6A, 12a.　　　　　TWO-LINE PICA MIKADO.　　　　　$8.85

We take pleasure in presenting this unique series To your Notice, believing you will agree with us In saying it is one of the Most Serviceable Letters yet Produced for Commercial and Ornamental Printing.　15 Ornamental Characters

4A, 4A, 8a.　　　　　THREE-LINE PICA MIKADO.　　　　　$10.65

Old Time is a droll wag Who puzzles the World with Rules, He can give to-day to the wise But the Morrow is Promised. $234.58 of Legal Money

3A, 3A, 6a.　　　　　FOUR-LINE PICA MIKADO.　　　　　$12.50

Our Greeting to Everyone Something New Each Day 18 Commercial Job Printers

CLEVELAND TYPE FOUNDRY 147 ST. CLAIR ST.

Freak Series.

PATENT APPLIED FOR.

12 A 25 A	10 POINT FREAK (Long Primer)	$2 75

American Coast Steamers

The ✦ United ✦ States ✦ Minister ✦ to ✦ France

23 ✦ Lower House of Congress ✦ 45

9 A 18 a	12 POINT FREAK (2 line Nonp.)	$2 85

Little Fisher Maiden

Sung ✦ at ✦ the ✦ Columbia ✦ Theatre

45 ✦ Splendid Music ✦ 67

6 A 12 a	18 POINT FREAK (3 line Nonp.)	$3 35

Chicago ✦ National ✦ Base ✦ Ball ✦ League

59 In Our Annual Struggle for Glory

Superior Copper-Mixed Type.   Great Western Type Foundry.

Barnhart Bros. & Spindler

✦ ✦ Letter Founders ✦ ✦

No. 115-117 Fifth Avenue   Chicago Illinois

5 A 10a	24 POINT FREAK (4 line Nonp.)	$3 95

Beautiful Christmas Attractions

In Novel Styles of Type 67

A 8a	30 POINT FREAK (5 line Nonp.)	$4 50

Spirits of the Long Departed ✦ ✦

✦ ✦ 38 Wafted Homeward

Manufactured by BARNHART BROS. & SPINDLER, Chicago.

Ferdinand

MECHANICAL PATENT, MARCH 31, 1885.

3 A, 5 a. 60 POINT FERDINAND. $9.85

Harlequinade

Frolicsome
Recreative

4 A, 10 a. 36 POINT FERDINAND. $5.30

Convulsed with Laughter
Amusing the Overworked with Burlesque
Scaramouch Performances
1234567890

Knowledge and
Genius avoiding

3 A, 8 a. 48 POINT FERDINAND. $7.35

Beaten Tracks

ALL COMPLETE WITH FIGURES.

The MacKellar, Smiths & Jordan Co., { 606-614 Sansom Street, Philadelphia.
Western Branch: 328-330 Dearborn St., Chicago.

SHEPARD SCRIPT SERIES.

Originated by THE CRESCENT TYPE FOUNDRY, 349 & 351 Dearborn Street, Chicago.

4A. 8a. 48 POINT SHEPARD SCRIPT $8.00

All Careful Employers

Steel Plate and Letter Press Printers

Efforts of Atlanta People

5A. 12a. 36 POINT SHEPARD SCRIPT $6.75

Some Departures in Type Founding

Many Beautiful Original Designs Shown Here

Glad Holiday Festivities Coming

6A. 18a. 24 POINT SHEPARD SCRIPT $5.25

May We Still Remember to Celebrate Christmas

Resort to Every Method to Introduce the Standard Lining System

Meritorious Efforts Should be Appreciated

8A. 18a. 18 POINT SHEPARD SCRIPT $3.75

The Attention of Printers and the Trade is Called to This New Face

It Being the First Script Ever Made on the Standard Line, Point System and Unit Set

Is Neat and Appropriate for All Classes of Fine Work

KEPT IN STOCK AND FOR SALE BY THE FOLLOWING FIRMS:

INLAND TYPE FOUNDRY, St. Louis, Mo.
KEYSTONE TYPE FOUNDRY, Philadelphia.
PACIFIC STATES TYPE FOUNDRY, San Francisco.

GOLDING & Co., Boston, New York, Chicago.
CONNER, FENDLER & Co., New York.
DOMINION PRINTERS SUPPLY Co., Toronto, Can.

Image Sources

Unless noted, all images reproduce items in the authors' collections.

Arts of the Book Collection, Arts Library, Yale University
(photographs by Robert Wright)
figures 2, 4, 23, 25, 26, 75, 78, 87
specimens 5, 7, 16–18, 23, 42, 43, 46, 50, 52–54, 56, 59

Collection of Bowne & Co. Stationers, South Street Seaport
pages 12, 34 (background photograph, Doug Clouse)
figures 15, 16, 21, 24, 36 (photograph, Doug Clouse), 58, 66, 69, 82, 90
specimens 9, 11–13, 26, 37

Brown University Library
specimens 47 and 48

The Grolier Club of New York
figures 64, 83
specimens 4, 6, 10, 14, 19, 22, 30, 31, 33, 36, 44, 51, 58

Kansas State Historical Society.
(photograph by L. W. Halbe)
page 10

Library of Congress
Prints and Photographs Division
figures 102, 104, 107
Rare Book and Special Collections Division
figure 5

Musée de l'imprimerie Lyon
figure 100

Museum of the City of New York, Byron Collection
figure 96

The New York Public Library
figures 19, 68
specimens 21, 32, 41, 49

Collection of Pat Reilly
page 2
specimen 8

Collection of Stephen O. Saxe
(photographs by Paul D'Agostino)
pages 9, 13, 50 (inset), 208
figures 9, 14, 34, 57, 59, 60, 65
specimens 15, 24, 27, 40, 45, 57, 60

Syracuse University Library, Ronald G. Becker Collection of
Charles Eisenmann Photographs, Special Collections Research Center
page 178

Courtesy Paul Tucker
figure 30

Collection of Robert Tuggle and Paul Jeromack,
Courtesy Munson-Williams-Proctor Arts Institute
(photograph by John Bigelow Taylor)
figure 13

Courtesy Vintage Catalogs,
© 2008, Vintage Catalogs. Reproduced with permission from the publisher
figure 31

Collection of Robert Warner
figure 8

Courtesy John Werry, RareVictorian.com
figure 29

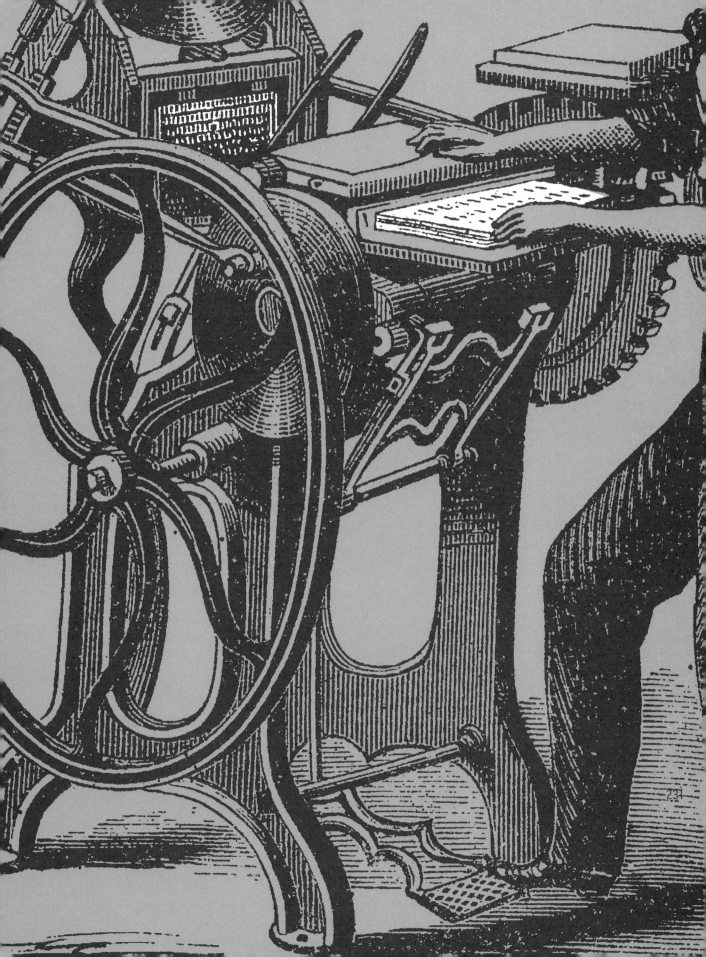

ISN'T THIS A DANDY?